VOTING FOR ETHICS

Markkula Center
for Applied Ethics
at Santa Clara University

VOTING FOR ETHICS

A Guide for U.S. Voters
Second Edition

John P. Pelissero • Ann G. Skeet
• Hana S. Callaghan

PALMETTO
PUBLISHING
Charleston, SC
www.PalmettoPublishing.com

Copyright © 2024 by Markkula Center for Applied Ethics

All rights reserved

No portion of this book may be reproduced, stored in a retrieval system, or transmitted in any form by any means–electronic, mechanical, photocopy, recording, or other–except for brief quotations in printed reviews, without prior permission of the author.

Paperback ISBN: 979-8-8229-5359-8
eBook ISBN: 979-8-8229-5360-4

TO:

Hana S. Callaghan

1956 - 2020

And keeping the ethical voting movement alive.

CONTENTS

About the Authors ix

Acknowledgements x

Preface xi

Introduction xvii

    Chapter 1: *Political Campaigning: Take The High Road* 1

    Chapter 2: *Political Communications Should Be Honest And Ethical* 9

    Chapter 3: *Campaign Finances: Raise And Spend Money The Right Way* . 23

    Chapter 4: *Promoting An Ethical Campaign Culture* 33

    Chapter 5: *A Practice Of Ethical Leadership* 39

    Chapter 6: *Artificial Intelligence In The Ethical Campaign* 49

    Chapter 7: *Ethical Candidates Support The Rule Of Law* 63

    Chapter 8: *What You Can Do To Encourage Ethical Campaigns* 77

Conclusion 87

Endnotes 89

Appendix A 109

Appendix B 119

Appendix C 123

Appendix D 129

ABOUT THE AUTHORS

John P. Pelissero is director of government ethics at the Markkula Center for Applied Ethics of Santa Clara University. A professor emeritus of political science at Loyola University Chicago, he taught American politics, state and urban politics, and public administration courses for 40 years. He is coauthor with Robert E. England and David R. Morgan of *Managing Urban America,* 8th ed. (CQ Press, 2016).

Ann G. Skeet is senior director of leadership ethics at the Markkula Center for Applied Ethics of Santa Clara University. A former media and nonprofit executive, Ann has studied the dilemmas of leaders and followers in her 10 years at the Center and in her role as CEO of American Leadership Forum-Silicon Valley. She was a contributor to the 1st edition of *Voting for Ethics* and also to Hana Callaghan's book, *Campaign Ethics.* Ann is also a co-author with Brian Green and José Flahaux of *Ethics in the Age of Disruptive Technologies: An Operational Roadmap.*

Hana S. Callaghan was director of government ethics at the Markkula Center for Applied Ethics of Santa Clara University from 2014 to 2020. She wrote the first edition of this book (2020) and *Campaign Ethics: A Field Guide* (2018). She was a leader in the ethical political campaign movement.

ACKNOWLEDGEMENTS

One cannot write and produce a book of any value without the assistance of others. That is true in the case of writing the second edition of *Voting for Ethics*. First, we must thank Hana Callaghan's husband, Michael, for his permission and encouragement to keep her ethical campaign movement alive through this new edition of her book. We want to recognize the professional advice of our Markkula Center colleagues who took time to inform our work: David DeCosse, Irina Raicu, and Subbu Vincent. We thank Joel Dibble and Debbie Dembecki from the center's public relations and marketing staff for formatting the final contents, and managing the relationship with Palmetto Publishing. We are grateful to Santa Clara student, Jessie Jiang, for designing the book's cover. We owe a debt of gratitude to Lee Hood, associate professor of broadcast journalism at Loyola University Chicago, for her excellent copyediting and advice on the manuscript and to Palmetto Publishing for their efforts to help us bring this work to fruition. And we appreciate the ongoing support of the Markkula Center's leaders, Don Heider, executive director, and Thor Wasbotten, managing director, who found the resources to allow this book to be produced. Of course, any errors or omissions are entirely our responsibility.

- J.P.P.
- A.G.S.

PREFACE

Ethics is an optimistic pursuit. To believe a movement for ethical candidates and campaigns could take hold in the United States in 2020, particularly in light of the events that followed it, exemplifies such optimism. That is what Hana Callaghan believed and why she wrote this book and another, *Campaign Ethics: A Field Guide*, that was published in 2018. It was a privilege to work with her on both.

Given Hana's duties in government ethics at the time, and mine in leadership ethics, we found plenty to talk about since we came to the center, a month apart, in 2014. We traded leadership war stories, she from her past perch in government, me from my experiences in business and the nonprofit sector. We bonded early on about how different it was to work in the academy than in some of our previous enterprises.

Hana served as the campaign manager for the Honorable Tom Campbell when he was a member of the United States House of Representatives. This gave her a front row seat to governing and campaigning and an understanding of the differences between the two. From the beginning, though she had plenty to say about governing across the spectrum, her passion was campaign ethics. She worked hard to make it a priority at the Ethics Center and for the constituents we serve on campus, here in Silicon Valley, and well beyond.

There are lots of ways someone working in government ethics could be spending her time as there are enough political and legal matters to study, opine, and teach, on a range of topics. Hana had the legal mind and the political savvy to do anything in her area of scholarship. She chose to make campaign ethics the centerpiece of her work. In spite of all the data provided the voting public to the contrary, Hana believed we could return to a time when the character of a candidate was a critical factor in electability, when campaigns were run with honor and focused on the future a candidate was trying to shape, rather than by trading barbs on the campaign trail and getting mired in the past.

Hana always looked to the future. She was no doubt doing so when she printed one last copy of this book on the day she died suddenly in January 2020 of a pulmonary embolism, as one of the most anticipated election years in our country's history began. It was inconceivable to stare down the year to come in campaign ethics at the start of 2020 and imagine doing so without her. And, it is inconceivable to me, even though it has been several years since, that we experienced the realities of the 2020 election and its aftermath without Hana's wisdom. But, vintage Hana, she left us well prepared for those events by sharing her insights and hope for a more ethical political future in this book.

Hana believed that we needed a movement for ethical campaigns. So she started one.

She went about this effort as she went about everything in her life, with joy. Her colleague and former boss, Tom Campbell, captured the essence of Hana at work for the people and with her joy, in a letter he wrote to her husband, Michael, and her adult sons, Grant and Chad, after her death.

> "Above all the attributes that appropriately describe her, joyful is the one I most wish to identify. Hana brought joy to everyone with whom she interacted. When a constituent presented herself or himself at our district office, or at one of our town hall meetings, with a problem, Hana would address it conscientiously and professionally. Whoever met with Hana was better off for it. But it was not her ability to deal with the substance of a problem that

I remember as the strongest aspect of her character. Of course, a constituent who met with Hana came away with the knowledge that she or he was respected and listened to, but also, the constituent actually left more joyful after a conversation with Hana. It was impossible not to share in Hana's joy. To Hana, life was joyful. Even a constituent caught in the gears of a slowly moving government, or deeply troubled by the course our country was taking, would, after talking with Hana, share in a bit of her joy.

I saw this happen time after time, as Hana and I drove together to town hall meetings in our Congressional district. We spent many hours together driving throughout Santa Clara and Santa Cruz counties going to the venues of our meetings with constituents. If a resident of our Congressional District cared enough to come to a town hall meeting, then Hana cared enough to treat her or him with respect and understanding. But she also conveyed to each person her remarkable, unique gift for happiness. She was convinced that we can choose to approach life with happiness, even under difficult personal circumstances. That perception, more than the resolution of any specific problem an individual was having with the federal government, was Hana's greatest gift.

And it affected me, too. Hana inspired me. She made me realize the tremendous honor it was to represent the people of our Congressional District. As a legal scholar, Hana loved to talk about US Constitutional issues. We often discussed that the founders intended Members of the House to be the federal officers closest to the people. Of all federal officials, only House Members were directly elected under our Constitutional system, as it was originally created. Hana reminded me that it was an honor, a responsibility, and a joy to be the representative of three quarters of a million Californians."

Hana derived meaning from the support she gave to other people. As her husband remarked in remembering her, she was the most other-centered person he knew. Whether you were her husband, children, daughter-in-law or grandchildren, Allison and

James; the lifelong girlfriends she made at Cal; the students she guided through their Hackworth Fellowships; or other scholars, public servants, and statesmen she worked with and for along the way—she was always in your corner.

Now, we have the opportunity to continue our support for Hana and her work as she supported us, with joy and intention, to take this book and its resources with us in the lives we will live as voters and to keep it current, just as Hana would have done.

The goals of Hana's movement for campaign ethics were straightforward: decrease political polarity by eliminating negative rhetoric, restore public trust in government, and increase civic engagement by providing better information to voters and healthier campaign conditions, so that more people intent on serving the common good, rather than themselves, would run for office.

Hana had confidence in voters. She believed we were smart, capable of applying our good judgment to the important issues of the day, and willing to do the work required to fully engage in democracy. She recognized such engagement as a right and a responsibility. She wrote this book to give us the tools we need and help us to recognize our accountability for the process of electing our representatives.

It's up to us, we voters, to keep Hana's ethical campaign movement going.

It is in the spirit of keeping the movement going that I return to contribute to and edit a second edition of this book, now working with the Markkula Center's next director of government ethics, John Pelissero. John is also a professor emeritus of political science at Loyola University Chicago, where he served on the faculty for 35 years until 2020. He is an accomplished researcher and teacher in various areas of American politics and has published two books on urban politics and urban management. In addition to his work in the classroom and as a researcher, John has more than 20 years of experience as a leader in higher education, serving as department chair for the Department of Political Science, associate provost and vice provost for academic affairs, seven years as provost and chief academic officer, and as Loyola University Chicago's interim president for one year.

John and I fully support Hana's belief that it will take a movement to positively shape the future of American politics, particularly the campaign and election experience. We approached our work to update *Voting for Ethics* with Hana's optimism, in spite of developments on the political scene that raise concerns.

To acknowledge those concerns, we have added two chapters. The first explores the implications of the widespread use of artificial intelligence (AI) in our society and the second revisits the events following the 2020 election, when its results were contested by one of the candidates, a sitting President, culminating in the unsettling events of January 6, 2021. One cannot adequately prepare for the 2024 elections without acknowledging the effects of these two experiences on American voters.

In light of these developments, it will take not only optimism, but an even greater commitment on the part of American voters to ethical elections. This book is our contribution to that commitment.

Ann Gregg Skeet
Santa Clara University

INTRODUCTION

There will be no end to the troubles of states, or of humanity itself, till philosophers become kings in this world, or till those we now call kings and rulers really and truly become philosophers, and political power and philosophy thus come into the same hands.

PLATO

Do you recall the quote from the movie "Network," where the lead character, Howard Beale, exclaims, "I'm mad as hell and I'm not going to take it anymore!"? That is how many of us feel about the current state of political campaigns, and we want to change that narrative.

Since politicians don't seem willing to rein themselves in, and voters increasingly struggle to agree upon a common set of facts, we at the Markkula Center for Applied Ethics wondered how the electorate can take back our political process and encourage ethical behavior on the campaign trail. We decided that the solution is an ethical campaign movement designed to let politicians know that we, the voters, want them to conduct civil and ethical campaigns. As part of that initiative we have written this short guide that will give voters tools to identify ethical candidates and strategies for encouraging ethical campaigning.

In 2016, the presidential race was seen as one of the dirtiest in American history. Donna Brazile, a CNN contributor and recent former chair of the Democratic National Committee, leaked primary debate questions to Hillary Clinton prior to the CNN-sponsored event.[1] Clinton called Donald Trump supporters "Deplorables."[2] Trump accused Ted Cruz's father of participating in the assassination of President Kennedy.[3] Clinton supporters were fraudulently informed that they didn't have to go to the polls – that they could vote by text instead.[4] Cruz sent out deceptive official-looking voter report cards intimidating voters into casting a ballot for him.[5] Marco Rubio taunted Trump about having "small hands."[6] DNC operatives started fights at GOP rallies.[7] Someone posted nude photos of Melania Trump.[8] WikiLeaks hacked and released DNC emails, and Russia meddled in our election by, among other things, producing a flood of fraudulent news stories on social media.[9] The name-calling and mudslinging left many of us disgusted, frustrated and turned off from civic engagement.

And that was all before the 2020 election.

Nothing could have prepared the electorate for the spectacle the 2020 election cycle became. For the first time in modern history, the peaceful transfer of power was threatened when sitting President Donald Trump challenged the results of elections through a series of acts intended to reverse the election's outcome. Those efforts came to a head in a violent attack on the United States Capitol as Congress was meeting to certify the election results.

As recently as June 2023, a Monmouth University poll found that "three-in-10 Americans still believe President Joe Biden won his 2020 election only due to voter fraud…a durable number that highlights the disconnect on one of the foundational issues facing American democracy."[10] The result is a deepening partisan divide over facts. "Virtually all Democrats (93%) say Biden won the election fairly, a view shared by 58% of independents. Just 21% of Republicans believe Biden won his election fair and square, while 68% say he won, 'due to vote fraud.'"[11]

Our process for electing public officials is born out of the ethical ideal of creating an informed electorate. But if the electorate cannot even agree on which information to believe, what does that mean for future elections? Irrelevant, misleading, and vitriolic campaign communications leave us without any real information about where a candidate stands. And misleading communications about election results leave us without the forward-looking reality usually accepted the day after an election: one candidate emerges with a mandate provided by the voters. In a vote that is questioned, that mandate is shaky enough to affect how the winner governs, and certainly how voters encounter future elections.

Fortunately, we have had the 2022 midterm elections since 2020 and, through them, have been able to restore some of the norms and confidence experienced by voters in previous elections. But as the 2023 Monmouth polling numbers reveal, an underlying disconnect between the facts and some voters remains.

Ethical lapses during campaigns do give us important information: they are a good indicator of how a person will govern once in office. At the campaign level, when candidates incur secret obligations in exchange for endorsements, we don't know to whom the candidate is beholden. In addition, the amount of money being contributed to or on behalf of political campaigns has never been greater, leaving us with the suspicion that politicians are more interested in representing their big donors than they are in representing the rest of us.

Many citizens are also frustrated by political polarity and the resultant lack of legislative productivity. We perceive that negotiation and compromise are no longer tools available for those who govern due to obligations created during the campaign process. Moreover, unethical political attacks freely dispensed during a campaign can poison later legislative relationships.

Statistics show that whereas voter turnout in the U.S. has improved since 2018, public trust in government is at historic lows.[12] According to the Bipartisan Policy Center, 57 percent of the electorate turned out to vote in 2016.[13] But in subsequent midterm elections (2018 and 2022) and in the 2020 presidential election, voter turnout began to grow and buck the downward trends of prior elections. According to the Pew Research Center, nearly 66 percent of voters turned out to cast a ballot in the 2020 presidential election, the highest turnout in over 100 years. With an increase in voter participation in the 2018 and 2022 midterm elections, these elections represent "…three of the highest-turnout U.S. elections of their respective types in decades."[14]

Nonetheless, voting in the United States trails most developed democracies in going to the polls. In another report from the Pew Research Center, the U.S. places 31 out of 49 in voting among OECD democracies based upon elections held between 2018-2022.[15] Even with the improved turnout of recent U.S. elections, our country still has a way to go to measure up to voter participation in other democracies around the globe.

At the Markkula Center for Applied Ethics we believe that one of the reasons for this civic disengagement is that our political process turns a blind eye toward unethical campaign practices. We believe that encouraging ethical campaigns will have three important benefits:

- It will help decrease political polarity by reducing the rancor in political races.

- It will help restore public trust in government by ensuring fairness and integrity in campaigns.

- It will help increase civic engagement by creating a process that not only encourages an informed and involved electorate but also encourages good people to run for office.

Research conducted by the Center for Campaign Leadership at the University of California-Berkeley and the Institute for Global Ethics shows that voters want to vote for the candidate who takes the high road – the one who tells the truth, is forthright about where they stand on issues, is independent, and doesn't engage in dirty, attack-style politics.[16] But how do we encourage candidates to campaign ethically? By letting our votes speak for us. All things being equal, we need to send a message to candidates that the ethical campaigner is the one who will get our vote. In order to do that, however, we first must be able to identify ethical candidates and learn what steps we can take as voters to encourage ethical behavior in campaigning and elections.

CHAPTER 1

POLITICAL CAMPAIGNING: TAKE THE HIGH ROAD

Politics is supposed to be the second-oldest profession. I have come to realize that it bears a very close resemblance to the first.

RONALD REAGAN

Observers of the U.S. political system know that dirty tricks in politics are nothing new. John Adams once feared that the Continental Congress would be ruled "...by noise, not sense; by meanness, not greatness; by ignorance, not learning; by contracted hearts, not large souls."[17] Thomas Jefferson supporters were told that they couldn't vote for Jefferson because he had died.[18] Teddy Roosevelt called candidate William Howard Taft "a fathead" with "the brains of a guinea pig."[19] In the modern era, the most infamous deployment of dirty tricks occurred when President Richard Nixon employed a group of "White House plumbers" to break into the headquarters of the Democratic National Committee at the Watergate building and employed dirty tricks throughout his 1972 reelection campaign.[20]

Taking the high road in political campaigns means that candidates must reject the use of dirty tricks and strive to run an ethical campaign. Candidates for office who pursue the high road will place the public interest above their political interests. They will campaign on the ethical virtues of truth, fairness, and integrity, even if they are told that using a dirty trick will gain them some political advantage. Taking the high road means demonstrating through the campaign's messaging, political tactics, and voter outreach that sharing the facts and truth with voters is the best way to conduct a campaign and win an election.

But aside from its inherent ugliness, dirty campaigning makes governing much harder. As noted by CNN contributor Bob Greene in 2012, and demonstrated time and again, the problem with scorched earth politics is that it is difficult to shift from mud wrestler to statesman once the votes have been counted.[21] Campaign dirty tricks have abounded, even after the Watergate scandal of 1972. Many observers by 2016 came to believe that politics is a dirty game that had gotten worse in the presidential campaign of that year and had sunk to a new low, reducing voters' trust in both political campaigns.[22]

It got worse in 2020, when Donald Trump, the incumbent president seeking reelection (and losing), sought to denigrate his opponent and family members, reporters, and even individuals who seemed to disagree with the president's views. Unfortunately, as the campaign of 2020 went on, Vice President Joe Biden resorted to telling President Trump to "shut up" during a debate, an act of frustration and one among a series of low points in the 2020 presidential debates.[23] We are also seeing an increase in polarity in the governing process, a direct result of the incivility born during nasty campaign battles. Legislative relationships poisoned during a campaign are hard to mend and make it difficult for later negotiation and compromise. In a recent Gallup Poll, only 28 percent of respondents were satisfied with the way our democracy is working, a record low[24] that threatens trust required for the legitimacy of our national government.

Even though negative campaigning and dirty tricks get wide

coverage in the press, there are stories of candidates whose conduct can provide good examples of what to look for in an ethical campaign.

In 1964, three weeks before the election, President Lyndon Johnson's aide (a married man) was arrested on a "morals charge" for having sex with another man in a YMCA changing room. Barry Goldwater's campaign staff urged the Republican presidential candidate to make an issue out of the arrest in the campaign. Goldwater refused. He was adamant that it wasn't relevant to the race, and he didn't want to participate in the character assassination of the Johnson staffer.[25]

In 2000, former congressman Tom Downey, the debate coach for Democratic nominee Al Gore, received in the mail a video of rival candidate George W. Bush's debate prep along with briefing materials. When Downey realized this material belonged to the Bush campaign, he turned it over to the FBI. Although he had only glanced at the materials briefly to determine their contents, he stepped down from the debate prep team "in order to ensure the integrity of the debate process."[26]

In 2008, presidential candidate Senator John McCain corrected a supporter in a town hall meeting who said she couldn't vote for Barack Obama because he was "an Arab." McCain responded, "No, ma'am. He's a decent family man [and] citizen that I just happen to have disagreements with on fundamental issues, and that's what this campaign's all about. He's not [an Arab]."[27] He told the jeering crowd, "I have to tell you, Senator Obama is a decent person and a person you don't have to be scared of as president of the United States." At Senator McCain's funeral, Barack Obama relayed this story and said, "[T]hat was John's instinct. I never saw John treat anyone differently because of their race or religion or gender. That in those moments that have been referred to during the campaign he saw himself as defending America's character, not just mine. He considered it the imperative of every citizen that loves this country to treat all people fairly."[28]

And who can forget Ronald Reagan's brilliant comeback to comments about his advanced age during a 1984 debate with Walter Mondale. With a shrug and a smile Reagan said, "I want you to know that I will not make age an issue of this campaign. I am not going to exploit for political purposes my opponent's youth and inexperience." Instead of attacking in kind, Reagan's ability to deflect earned him the reputation of being a likeable guy—and helped him win a second term.[29]

Michelle Obama made an important statement about how to respond to unethical campaign tactics in her 2016 rallying cry to the Democratic Convention, "When they go low, we go high,"[30] which should be the guiding mantra for all ethical candidates, regardless of party. It was a call for campaigns to respond to dirty tricks and the gutter style of politics by projecting a positive approach to campaigns that sets a high standard for decency and ethical behavior.

As the 2024 presidential election begins, we already have dirty tricks in play, some made easier by the availability of generative artificial intelligence (AI). We speak more thoroughly to the issue of AI in campaigns and how to deploy such responsibly in Chapter 6. It is reasonable to worry about AI's misuse in political campaigns because we don't know exactly how this technology will change the campaign environment and we are seeing instances of irresponsible use of AI in this election. For instance, in the very first Republican primary in New Hampshire in January 2024, AI was used to "deep fake" voters into believing they were receiving a robocall from President Biden urging them not to vote in the primary election.[31]

DIRTY TRICKS

As we have noted earlier, dirty tricks have been around political campaigns for centuries. What constitutes a dirty trick and why are these unethical in campaigns? The following are examples of dirty tricks to look out for when evaluating the ethics of a campaign:

Whisper Campaigns

Conducting a whisper campaign is an unfair tactic whereby rumors, innuendo, and slanderous statements are quietly conveyed in order to damage reputations and/or dry up funding sources and support. The negative assertions are not made publicly; thus, the subject may have no idea about what is being said until it is too late. Also, because the allegations are not made publicly, the target is caught in a Catch-22: if the candidate publicly denounces the rumors, it calls attention to the issue. If the candidate ignores the behind-the-back rumors, the campaign can be damaged. It is a tough position to be in. The ethical candidate will decide whether or not to respond to such rumors based on what is in the best interests of voters. If the rumors are causing genuine confusion, they likely need to be addressed.

Push Polling

Push polling is an unfair and unethical political device used to communicate negative messages. A push poll is one where, under the guise of conducting a legitimate poll, defamatory or otherwise negative and usually false information is conveyed. The American Association of Political Consultants condemns this practice, declaring on their website, "Push-polls violate the AAPC's stricture against 'any activity which would corrupt or degrade the practice of political campaigning.' To the extent that practitioners of the 'push-poll' ruse convey inaccurate information about an election opponent, they also violate the AAPC's stricture against false and misleading attacks."[32]

Unfair Competition

Practices that hamper the opponent's ability to fairly compete are unethical. For example, you will sometimes see wealthy candidates hiring as many political consultants as are available, not for their services, but to keep them from working for the opponent.

If a candidate condones unfair political practices, such as the removal of posters, or any behavior that stifles the opponent's message, they are engaging in unethical campaigning. While it may be easy to shrug this conduct off as "campaign shenanigans," in reality it is the suppression of political speech. Ethical campaigns help create an informed electorate. Stifling speech does just the opposite. A candidate who allows staff and supporters to act in such a manner will be seen as standing for what they condone.

Interference with the Electoral Process

Any campaign practice that provides an obstacle to a citizen's ability to vote interferes with our democratic notions of fair and free elections. Such practices are not only unethical but are in many instances illegal. Destruction of mail-in ballots, deliberately staged traffic jams on Election Day, and voter intimidation at the polls are all examples of unethical—and illegal—tactics designed to discourage voting. So, too, are messages that polling places are "too crowded" to be able to cast a ballot or that the election has already been decided while voters are on their way to vote. On the flip side, it is also unethical and illegal to incentivize voter turnout for a particular candidate by offering a reward or free gifts for voting. Voting is a privilege freely exercised and cannot be bought. More examples of voter interference are discussed in Chapter 7.

The October Surprise

The infamous "October surprise" is the generic term for a negative attack that comes out shortly before an election (which is commonly in November), giving the target of the attack little or no time to respond. If the attack is subject to denial or rational explanation, the interests of an informed electorate require that assertions be timed in such a way as to allow response. You as a voter should be able to make decisions based on all the information available, not just the information provided by one side.

AI-Generated Deep Fakes

By the advent of the 2024 election cycle, dirty tricks involved the misuse of generative AI to trick voters into believing something that is not true. This includes AI-generated images and audio intended to make voters believe they are seeing or hearing a candidate promoting a message that is actually false. It can also be "fake news" that is circulated to influence people's beliefs, often directing them away from credible media to true fakes. We should be watchful of AI's deployment to shape the outcomes of elections. Using technology to mislead, misinform, or confuse voters is unethical and voters need to be sure that they are aware of this possibility.[33] More on AI is found in Chapter 6.

Most voters want candidates to take the high road and eschew dirty tricks in political campaigns. Knowing when and where misinformation presents itself and how to assess the truthfulness and accuracy of news, information, communications, and candidates is more challenging in the age of AI. But it remains an important ideal for voters to seek the ethical nature of candidates and their campaigns in order to make an informed choice on election day.

TAKEAWAYS

Here are five things to look for when judging ethical political engagement:

1. *Does the candidate show respect for the opponent and for the political process?*

2. *Is the candidate always truthful about their record and about the opponent's record?*

3. *Does the candidate strive to keep their message about the issues?*

4. *Does the candidate take the high road and reject dirty tricks in their campaign?*

5. *Does the candidate avoid communicating misinformation during the campaign?*

CHAPTER 2

POLITICAL COMMUNICATIONS SHOULD BE HONEST AND ETHICAL

If one morning I walked on top of the water across the Potomac River, the headline that afternoon would read: 'President Can't Swim.'

LYNDON JOHNSON

Election season is here and the campaign ad onslaught is upon us! For some of us, having a root canal would be better than being subjected to the seemingly endless stream of mud spewing from our televisions, computers and mobile phones. Political speech is afforded great protection under the First Amendment of the U.S. Constitution, so there is little regulators can do to improve the tenor of political ads. It is up to us to demand respectful and honest communications from our political candidates.

As noted before, ethical campaigns are those that serve to create an informed electorate. It follows, then, that ethical campaign communications are those designed to inform voters about matters pertinent to their voting decision(s). By communication we mean every aspect of political messaging – from ads, mailers, interviews, debate responses, to social media and campaign websites. It's the campaign's task to introduce the candidate and educate the voters about the candidate's background, his or her positions on the issues, and how the candidate is different from the opponent.

Even negative messaging about an opponent is ethical so long as the negative information is factual, relevant and necessary for the voters to make an informed decision.

Accordingly, responsible communications are those that convey truthful information about the candidate, about the opponent, and about the issues in the race. Ethical messaging also requires that the information being conveyed is fair and that it is relevant to the contest. Finally, in order to inform, the candidate must let voters know where they stand, including on the importance of the rule of law. Ethical campaigns have substantive policy positions to back up soundbites offered on the campaign trail. Here is a look at key standards for ethical campaign communications.

Truthfulness

Deceptive messaging violates the candidate's duty to inform the voter about the candidate's background, what the candidate stands for, and how the candidate's positions differ from that of the opponent. Telling lies to future constituents also reduces trust not only in our election process but in government in general.

Cornell University ethics professor Dana Radcliffe has identified why truth matters. He says, "From a moral point of view, what's wrong with deception is that it is a betrayal of trust. You cannot deceive someone unless they trust you, believing that you're being truthful with them. When you succeed in deceiving them, you exploit that trust, using that person for your own ends. In every domain of life, such betrayals weaken or destroy the trust relationships essential to our vital institutions, including (among others) marriage and family, business, education, and representative government."[34]

The good news for voters is that fact-checking organizations such as Politifact.com and Factcheck.org[35] provide ready access to the truth. In addition, we can easily engage in internet research for contemporaneous news articles to discover whether a candidate's view of historic events, such as the opponent's voting record, comports with the truth.

We also have a duty as engaged citizens to ascertain the truth of political communications before we forward those assertions on social media. We all know now that in the 2016 presidential election internet trolls from other countries created fake news stories on social media, which so many of us happily (and in blissful ignorance) passed on to our friends and family. We were, sadly, complicit in spreading the lies.

The importance of truthfulness has suffered some serious setbacks since the 2016 elections. Perhaps the most significant threat to the truth is what came to be known as the "big lie" after the 2020 presidential election. When Joseph Biden was declared the winner of the presidential general election, Donald Trump, the incumbent president who lost the election, and many of his campaign officials and supporters, promulgated the false claim that the election had been stolen.[36] Despite the lack of evidence of a stolen election or any significant level of fraud, the big lie is still repeated in 2024 and, sadly, many in the Republican Party continue to believe that this falsehood is the truth.[37]

Voters interested in furthering the goal of increased truth in our political process might also consider taking the Pro-Truth Pledge, an initiative launched by a group of behavioral scientists hoping to increase truth in politics. The pledge provides:

I Pledge My Earnest Efforts To:

Share truth

☐ *Verify: Fact-check information to confirm it is true before accepting and sharing it*

- ☐ *Balance:* Share the whole truth, even if some aspects do not support my opinion
- ☐ *Cite:* Share my sources so that others can verify my information
- ☐ *Clarify:* Distinguish between my opinion and the facts

Honor truth

- ☐ *Acknowledge:* Acknowledge when others share true information, even when we disagree otherwise
- ☐ *Reevaluate:* Reevaluate if my information is challenged, retract it if I cannot verify it
- ☐ *Defend:* Defend others when they come under attack for sharing true information, even when we disagree otherwise
- ☐ *Align:* Align my opinions and my actions with true information

Encourage truth

- ☐ *Fix:* Ask people to retract information that reliable sources have disproved even if they are my allies
- ☐ *Educate:* Compassionately inform those around me to stop using unreliable sources even if these sources support my opinion
- ☐ *Defer:* Recognize the opinions of experts as more likely to be accurate when the facts are disputed
- ☐ *Celebrate:* Celebrate those who retract incorrect statements and update their beliefs toward the truth

For more information about the Pro-Truth Pledge please go to https://www.protruthpledge.org/

In order to run an ethical campaign, candidates must be vigilant that all communications by the candidate and by those authorized to speak for the candidate are free of deception. Look for campaigns that fact-check all assertions and have the evidence to back up their statements. Being truthful is an important virtue that we should expect to be present in an ethical campaign's communications.[38]

Often, however, with the advent of ever more powerful independent expenditure committees, a message going out to voters might not be initiated by a campaign, but rather by an outside group. What should a candidate do in a situation where an outside group produces a communication that doesn't comport with the candidate's values?

Independent expenditure committees (known as I.E.s) are outside groups that support a candidate and create campaign ads either supporting the candidate or attacking the opponent. Campaigns don't have any control over the messaging by independent groups. In fact, it's against the law for campaigns to coordinate with I.E.s. In the U.S. Supreme Court's decision in *Citizens United v. F.E.C.* case in 2010, the court allowed corporations and other interests to spend significant amounts of money on candidates, a decision that has had a profound impact on political campaigns.[39]

Ethical candidates should at the very outset of the campaign announce their commitment to truthful and substantive advertising. If an I.E. issues a communication that doesn't live up to the candidate's standards, the ethical candidate should immediately and publicly disavow the ad or unethical campaign tactic.

Fairness

Going into a campaign, most people have a moral understanding that it is wrong to outright lie. The problem is, most candidates don't anticipate the ethical choices they will have to make about communications once the campaign is in full swing. Most campaign communications have at least a kernel of truth, but in the heat of the battle sometimes that kernel becomes wrapped in deception. We have all seen candidates succumb to the temptation to approve a communication that, while true on its face, creates an unfair inference. The following are examples of common unfair tactics to watch out for in political communications:

Facts Out of Context: The most common way in which campaigns stretch the truth is to take true facts out of context. The prime example of this is citing an opponent's roll call vote without the full history behind the vote. A legislator may truthfully have a record of voting a certain way on a certain policy; however, at some point they may have cast a vote that in a vacuum looks contrary to that policy. This vote may have occurred because the legislator did not believe that the bill went far enough to achieve the policy and so voted against it. Or, a legislator may have to compromise his or her stance on a particular policy in order to pass a larger comprehensive bill on an essential funding matter. Regardless of the reason, the legislator's opponent jumps on this isolated vote to proclaim that the legislator is against a prime issue in the race. In all these situations, what the opponent claimed was true—the candidate did vote a certain way on a certain date—however, the inference that the vote is reflective of the candidate's record on the issue is deceptive.

Statements Out of Context: Votes are not the only thing taken out of context. Often you will see ads quoting the opponent in a negative fashion. While it may be true that the candidate did say the words, the context of the quote may not justify the inference that the candidate is making about the opponent.

Deceptive Imagery: Visual imagery may also contribute to the deceptive nature of a communication. Even though the words are true, images are manipulated to falsely infer something negative about an opponent or something positive about the candidate. For example, you may have seen unrelated pictures in an ad abutted together to falsely infer a relationship between two people. This is called deceptive framing. Using this tactic, political ads often wrongly infer guilt by association when a candidate's picture is juxtaposed with the picture of someone presumably despised by the voters. The conclusion being prompted is that the opponent and the other pictured individual are ideologically aligned.

Photographic Alterations: Photo editing can be another way political consultants might blatantly manipulate images in a deceptive manner. For example, the candidate's image might be Photoshopped into a picture with a highly respected person, thereby implying an endorsement when none has actually been given. With the new capabilities provided by artificial intelligence, images known as "deepfakes" produce false images of people so that ads can easily mislead voters into believing candidates have said something they never did.

Visual Vilification: A regrettably favored tactic in a campaign is where a grossly unflattering photograph of an opponent is selected to underscore an attack and put the opponent in a bad light. You may ask why this is unethical. The answer is that a candidate's appearance has nothing to do with the issues of the race. By using unflattering photographs, the opponent is appealing to unconscious voter bias instead of informing voters about the issues.

Native Political Advertising: "Native advertising" is defined by the Native Advertising Institute as "paid advertising where the ad matches the form, feel and function of the content of the media on which it appears."[40] For example, a campaign might create a video that mimics the look of a television anchor delivering what appears to be a genuine news story. In other cases, campaigns have created "news" websites purporting to be an actual news outlet but with only sponsored content. These will also be easier to produce with artificial intelligence. The problem with these news-like videos, websites, and articles is that, unlike legitimate news stories, there is no independent investigation, no vetting of sources, no editors, and no unbiased reporting. By trying to pass these stories off as authentic news rather than political advertising, these campaigns are attempting to manufacture credibility. In other words, the pure intent of what is known as native political advertising is to deceive voters about the origin of the piece.

This type of advertising is not illegal, so long as the videos or articles are marked as paid for by the specific political committee. But, as is often the case, the disclaimer is difficult to find. It is also a problem when the content, once read, gets shared over and over on social media as legitimate news. Just because something is legal does not necessarily make it ethical. Attempting to deceive voters is always unethical, regardless of the legality.

Finally, note that Fairness is an important ethical standard in campaigns.

Relevance
We have talked about truth, and we have spoken about fairness. Now let's discuss relevance.

Since ethical communications must serve to inform the electorate about matters pertinent to their voting decision, it only follows that communications that are irrelevant to the issues facing voters are inappropriate. We have all seen attack ads that talk about a candidate's youthful indiscretions, private marital troubles, or problematic behavior on the part of a candidate's family member or associate.

The question of whether these types of attacks are relevant to the issues in the campaign is a tricky one. For example, we may not care if a politician is having an extramarital affair because it arguably has nothing to do with his or her capability to govern. However, if that same candidate is running on a family values platform, the issue of fidelity might suddenly become relevant because it demonstrates that the candidate is not being honest with us. As another example, the fact that a known associate of a candidate has been indicted might be unethically used to imply guilt by association. Unless there is some direct connection between the associate's wrongdoing, the candidate, and the issues in the race, the associate's wrongdoing is irrelevant to our voting decision and thus an improper topic for campaign rhetoric.

The motivation behind these negative attacks is germane to whether the attacks are ethical. You as a voter must ask yourself, are the spots designed purely to appeal to your emotions or inherent bias, or is the content in the ad pertinent to a legitimate interest that you care about in the race? Political Science Professor L. Sandy Maisel, in the essay "Candidates: Promises and Persuasion," advises candidates to ask themselves:

1. Why am I doing this?
2. Does the importance of the issue overweigh the costs I am inflicting on another person and family?
3. Does this issue really define the difference between me and my opponent on a criterion that the public should be using to judge us?[41]

We as voters should ask the same questions about the candidate's motivation and ethical decision making.

Maisel also proposes that candidates should consider the impact that negative attack ads have on democracy in general. Studies have shown that negative attacks not only have the intended effect of lowering trust in the target of the attack, but also have the consequence of lowering trust in the attacker. Maisel concludes, the overall result is increased public disapproval of politicians as a group and of the political process in general.[42]

Substance

There has been a troubling trend in recent years where candidates are advised to provide as little information as possible regarding their policy solutions. The purported idea is to allow the candidate's positions to evolve during the course of the campaign, which is hampered if the positions are "engraved in stone." The actual reason for being less than forthright about positions is to avoid creating a record of ideas with which the electorate can find fault. In other words, these candidates are being advised not to give their opponents ammunition they can use for an attack or a reason for voters to say no.

We as voters should demand substance, not sound bites, from those seeking office. Failure to disclose positions is the antithesis to the ideal of creating an informed electorate. At a minimum, candidates should be expected to reveal their positions on all major issues that are at stake during a political campaign. This way, voters will be able to assess the substance and solutions that a candidate would bring to an issue if elected.

Above all else, campaigns should be a clash of ideas, not a battle of personalities. The ethical campaign has substantive position statements presented on the campaign website. The ethical candidate responds in detail to interviewers and doesn't dodge debate questions. Many ethical candidates engage with their voters in town hall campaign events, taking questions from the audience.

They also create blog posts communicating directly to the voters about their ideas.

ETHICAL CAMPAIGN PROMISES

Ethical campaign promises should be realistic, clearly articulated, made with the intent to fulfill the promise, and capable of being accomplished. An ethical candidate doesn't make promises about something that they do not have the power to achieve. For example, a state legislator has limited authority in an area under the purview of the federal government and therefore can't make a promise to do something that is solely within the jurisdiction of Congress. As another example, a person in an executive position cannot promise to bring about a result that can only be achieved through legislation.

Candidates should only make promises that are achievable and relevant to the office that they seek. For example, candidates for federal offices should not make promises about how they would change local policies over which they have no control. A candidate running for president of the U.S. should not make statements or promises that are more appropriate for a candidate who is running for president of the local school board.

Ethical campaign promises should also be consistent. Candidates who promise one group one thing and another group the opposite lose all credibility and demonstrate a lack of integrity. In the days before the internet, social media, and the 24-hour news cycle, politicians may have been more able to get away with being "flexible" in their commitments. Today a politician who makes inconsistent promises will most likely find him- or herself explaining on the nightly news.

Where a campaign might be tempted to make inconsistent promises is when seeking endorsements from various interest groups. A current standard practice is for interest groups to require candidates to answer questionnaires prior to endorsing. In concept this is perfectly reasonable, as groups want to ensure that the candidate's interests are aligned with theirs prior to giving their support. However, candidate responses to questionnaires are often kept confidential – purportedly to allow the candidate to feel more comfortable answering. But when a campaign really needs an endorsement, secret responses provide the temptation to answer one way for one group of endorsers and entirely differently for another group.

Another problem with confidential questionnaire responses is that candidates are in essence creating secret obligations on matters about which voters have a right to know. Voters and the news media should demand that candidates make all responses to questionnaires public. If an endorsing group does not want their questions and the candidate's responses to be made known, it should give voters cause to question the endorser's – and the candidate's – motives to keep this knowledge from the voters. Are the endorsing groups creating an obligation that they know voters won't like but that can be used to put pressure on the candidate once in office?

TRUE, FAIR, AND RELEVANT: APPLYING THE CRITERIA

Hana Callaghan, who wrote the first edition of this book, was once asked to comment on a race for a law enforcement position where one candidate claimed that his opponent, a law enforcement officer, was caught up in a police sweep of a brothel in Las Vegas more than 11 years ago. Her recollection of this story is instructive on how one should apply the criteria of true, fair, and relevant to assessing a story that came up during a political campaign.[43]

My gut reaction was, "How awful! How could an officer of the law violate the law by visiting a house of prostitution?" Then I paused and thought to myself that before I let my gut make political decisions for me, I should run this charge through the same analysis I advise voters to make when deciding whether a political communication is ethical.

I researched the brothel story to see if it was true, fair, and relevant in order to determine if the charge was fair game in this political race. It turns out, the candidate had been caught up in a police sweep of a brothel in Las Vegas. So, it WAS true. Case closed? Not so fast.

Researching further, it turned out that the candidate was not inside the brothel, as claimed by his opponent. He never went inside. Rather, he was outside waiting for his boss. He was never charged with any crime. So, while it was true that he had been caught up in the sweep, the implication that he had violated the law was not fair.

Now knowing the facts, I asked myself, "Is it relevant to my voting decision whether 11 years before, the candidate exercised questionable judgment by waiting for his boss outside of a brothel?" The relevance question is truly a subjective one that each of us will answer differently. However, the ability to answer that question requires a knowledge of all the facts.

So, the next time you see a negative charge in a political race (and we promise you that in the weeks before any election you will), take a moment to do a little research. You may find that political accusations often tell you more about the ethics of the accuser than about the accused. And that is information you can use at the polls.

TAKEAWAYS

Here are five things to look for when assessing ethical campaign communications:

1. *Is the candidate truthful in their communications?*

2. *Are the candidate's statements fair in addition to being truthful?*

3. *Are the candidate's communications about topics that are relevant to the issues in the race?*

4. *Does the candidate help inform the electorate by developing substantive policy positions?*

5. *Does the candidate make promises that can be met?*

CHAPTER 3

CAMPAIGN FINANCES: RAISE AND SPEND MONEY THE RIGHT WAY

All elected officials would lead happier lives and be better able to perform their public responsibilities if they did not have to spend so much time raising money.[44]

JOHN PAUL STEVENS, former associate justice of the Supreme Court

More so than ever, political campaigns are expensive. A campaign must be able to get the candidate's name and message out to the people, and that takes money. Given our current campaign finance system, unless a candidate is a self-funder, they will have to ask others for contributions. Even self-funders sometimes ask for money because the press uses amounts raised by a campaign as an indication of a candidate's popularity. Debate organizations use fundraising numbers to determine whether a candidate qualifies to get on the debate stage. The old adage, "money begets money," was never as true as in political fundraising.

The problem with our current campaign finance system is that we generally distrust candidates who receive money from others, fearing that the mere fact of a political contribution creates a bias in favor of the contributor.[45] The fact that a candidate has received a contribution and later takes an official action in favor of the contributor may not be evidence in and of itself of corruption. However, the perception may linger with voters that by accepting a large donation from an individual or organization, the candidate may owe the donor something in return.

Most politicians are not corrupt. They are civic-minded people who want to enter public service and enact change for the common good. Regrettably, they are faced with the unenviable dilemma of having to "beg" for campaign contributions before they can help their communities. And because of this, they are vilified before they even begin. Incumbents intending to run for reelection to a two-year term typically must begin fundraising for the next election the very day that they win reelection. Put another way, incumbents in 2-year terms are constantly in reelection mode, including fund-raising throughout their short terms of office. How can you identify candidates who are fundraising honestly and spending campaign contributions properly? The following line of inquiry may help.

Does the Candidate Maintain Independence from Contributors?

Most candidates and elected officials don't engage in the type of quid pro quo politics where a candidate or official says to a donor, "If you give me money, I will do X for you personally." That, of course, would be illegal extortion. The flip side, when a contributor says, "If you do X for me, I will give you campaign funds," is also illegal. That's bribery. Although these illegal activities do occur, it's often in other more subtle and legal ways that money influences policy.[46] Accordingly, this is not an area where the law alone should inform actions, but also the candidate's ethics.

Public officials take on certain ethical duties when they enter public service, including the duty of impartiality.[47] This means they have an ethical responsibility to treat all constituents equally and fairly, not just those who donated to their campaign. Ethics requires that a candidate be willing to risk their financial relationships, and possibly the ability to get elected, by maintaining independence, not substituting their donors' judgment on issues for their own. Candidates must be committed to the public's interest alone, not to moneyed interests.

As a voter, watch out for any candidate who changes campaign positions not because of a heartfelt belief that the policy will serve the common good, but because the change in policy will result in campaign contributions. If the candidate is an office holder, determine whether they have a record of favoring donors over other constituents or are unduly influenced by donors in creating policy once elected. It's always possible that the public's interest and the donor's interest align, but that conclusion should only be reached after honest reflection on the official's true motivations.

It's helpful to have a framework to evaluate the candidate's actions. The Markkula Center for Applied Ethics has developed the "Framework for Ethical Decision Making," which has been used by professionals the world over. By posing a series of questions, the framework provides ethical filters for looking at ethical dilemmas. The framework can be found in the Appendices of this guide or online at https://www.scu.edu/ethics/ethics-resources/a-framework-for-ethical-decision-making/

Does the Candidate Manage Donor Expectations?
Since the common wisdom seems to be that "money talks" in politics, it should not be surprising when donors believe that their money

will "speak" to the candidate and successfully sway the candidate toward their point of view. What should you look for to determine if the candidate counters this belief by managing donor expectations?

Check to see if the candidate is forearmed with clearly articulated positions. The candidate should be prepared with substantive policy statements on the campaign website. The candidate's positions should be reinforced by consistent messaging in ads, campaign events, statements to the press, responses to debate questions, and answers to candidate questionnaires. Well-publicized policy objectives make it less likely for donors to believe the candidate will change their mind because of financial incentives.

How does the candidate ask for money? When making solicitations, the ethical campaign is clear that the only reason a person should contribute is that, on balance, the donor supports the candidate's policy objectives. For those matters yet to be anticipated, the candidate should use best judgment based on experience, knowledge, and values. A general statement on the campaign website regarding the candidate's philosophy on contributions is one indication that the candidate is educating donors about what they can expect. Another would be a friendly disclaimer on campaign solicitation materials that alerts donors to the fact that campaign contributions will not provide greater access or influence.

An *example of a disclaimer* might be:

Dear Friend,
We are grateful to you for your campaign contribution! By contributing you have joined your neighbors and friends who believe that together we can bring about a better future for our children. Your generous contribution will help pay for the campaign-related expenses necessary for our success on Election Day. Of course, no outcome is guaranteed, nor is greater access or influence promised as a result of a political contribution. What I do promise is to always

use my best judgment to take actions that are in the public interest and further the common good. Thank you for your belief in me.

The fact that a candidate sends a loud and clear message that they cannot be bought or influenced by contributions may be a helpful indicator that the candidate will be an independent, impartial public official once in office.

Does the Candidate Disclose Donor Information?

Voters may be distrustful of anonymous contributors. We want to know to whom a candidate is beholden and who might be trying to exert influence. If a candidate is afraid to be publicly aligned with a particular donor for fear it will hurt their chances with the general electorate, the candidate should not be tempted to take the contribution in the first place. Ethical campaigns hire professionals knowledgeable in the political reporting requirements governing the candidate's chosen office to make sure proper disclosures are made.

Ethical dilemmas regarding disclosure also arise when donations are not made directly to a candidate, but rather to an independent expenditure committee (I.E.) that indirectly supports the candidate.[48] "Individuals, political committees, Super PACs, qualified nonprofit corporations (such as 501(c)(4)'s) and, since Citizens United v. Federal Election Commission, corporations and labor unions are permitted to make independent expenditures."[49] Some independent expenditures are made by organizations that don't have to disclose their members.[50] It may be difficult for a candidate to know of the existence of an I.E. or the contributors to it. However, the candidate should always be forthright about the need for transparency in campaign finance and encourage disclosure on the part of any group raising money and acting on the candidate's behalf.

Does the Candidate Refrain from Using Public Resources for Campaigning?

An ethical dilemma peculiar to those candidates who already hold office is the temptation to use public resources to help defray campaign costs. Public officials have an ethical duty of loyalty[51] to the public they serve. This means they must put the public's interest before their personal political pursuits. Implicit in this ideal is the principle that a public official cannot use taxpayer-funded public resources for political gain. For example, a candidate cannot use government office space, equipment, vehicles, or email accounts for campaign-related activities. Nor should an official use any indicia of office, such as agency letterhead or the agency seal, on campaign materials. The same holds true for using official public meeting time as an opportunity to make a campaign speech.

An incumbent cannot use their government franking privilege or mass mailing budget for campaign purposes. In fact, many jurisdictions have restrictions on incumbent mass mailings or other official contact with voters – even for governmental reasons – close to an election. Other rules prevent images of uniformed law enforcement in campaign materials or commercials. Candidates who disregard these guidelines are showing they cannot be trusted with public resources.

Public officials must be careful when traveling for political campaign purposes, including their reelection bid. Officials may never use government resources, including transportation, offices, or office equipment for campaign purposes. One must use only campaign organization resources when running for reelection. Occasionally, senior government officials who are seeking reelection or another elected office must travel by government-paid transportation for reasons of official business or security. In such instances, the official must determine the fair cost of the campaign and election travel and reimburse the government for those expenditures.

Also, be wary about government staff participation in political campaigns. Government staffers owe their allegiance to the public that pays their salaries. They too are considered a public resource. They are hired to help all constituents, not just those who support the official's election. Some may argue, correctly, that staffers have an independent First Amendment right to support their boss's campaign if they wish. However, they must not be coerced into helping, and they must do so voluntarily on their own time and on their own dime. Because it is so easy for the lines to become blurred, many incumbents have a strong firewall between government and politics and don't allow their staff members to participate at all in their campaigns. You may want to give "extra credit" to a candidate with a thick wall, where there is no chance that staff will perceive any implied coercion.

It is also unethical for a candidate to ask government staff to contribute to their campaign. Staffers may feel an implied threat that if they don't contribute to their boss's campaign, they will lose their job. By soliciting campaign funds from staff, the official may be sending a message to employees that staff loyalties should be to the official first rather than to the public that they were hired to serve. Such contributions blur the line between a government staffer's duty to serve the public interest, rather than the political interest of an elected official.

Note too that it would be a misuse of public resources for a candidate to ask government staff to look into a matter that would benefit the campaign. A good practice, as stated by California's Institute for Local Government, is, if the candidate wouldn't ask staff to look into a matter if they weren't running for re-election, it isn't appropriate to ask staff to look into it when the candidate is.[52]

Is the Candidate a Good Steward of Donated Campaign Funds?

When people donate funds to a cause, be it a political campaign or a nonprofit, they expect the funds to be used to further the organization's mission. In the case of campaign contributions, the expectation is that the funds will be used for legitimate campaign operations to help get the candidate elected. That is why outrage erupts when contributors learn that their donations have been used for personal purposes such as for Botox treatments and lavish personal trips (of former Republican Congressman George Santos, who was eventually expelled from the House of Representatives[53]) or purchasing Michael Jackson memorabilia (the way Democrat Jesse Jackson Jr. did[54]).

When campaign funds are used for the candidate's personal benefit with the donor's permission, the appearance is that the funds are a blatant attempt to wield influence. The donation looks more like a gift (or a bribe) rather than a legitimate political contribution.

For these reasons, many jurisdictions have legislated parameters on appropriate campaign spending. For example, in California, expenditures of state campaign funds are highly regulated and must be "reasonably related to a political, legislative, or governmental purpose." The rules require, among other things, that mileage spent for travel is reimbursable if related to the campaign, but clothing is a personal expense and campaign funds generally cannot be used for attire. A campaign may use funds to purchase office equipment, but if it purchases any vehicles, the title must be held by the campaign committee. A campaign meal that is less than $200 can be reimbursed if "reasonably related" to a campaign activity. If the meal costs more than $200, there must be a direct connection between the meal and the campaign.[55] As you can see, these rules are very specific and can become quite complicated. If you think a candidate is violating campaign finance rules, consider contacting the agency overseeing campaign ethics laws in your jurisdiction—and consider withholding your support.

TAKEAWAYS

Here are five things to look for when assessing whether a candidate raises funds and pays for their campaign ethically:

1. *Does the candidate maintain independence from funders?*

2. *Does the candidate manage donor expectations?*

3. *Does the candidate disclose donors?*

4. *Does the candidate use public resources for political purposes?*

5. *Is the candidate a good steward of donated campaign funds?*

CHAPTER 4

PROMOTING AN ETHICAL CAMPAIGN CULTURE

It is a terrible thing to look over your shoulder when you are trying to lead and find no one there.

FRANKLIN ROOSEVELT

As with any organization, it is important for the leaders to set the ethical tone at the top. In the campaign setting, the leaders are the candidate, campaign manager, strategic political consultants, and senior staff. To see if a campaign organization is being run ethically, it's useful to know if the candidate has articulated a clear set of standards by which the campaign is to be run. The campaign leaders need to model the ethical behavior that the standards represent. The campaign leaders should make it known that the standards are applicable to all staff, volunteers, and anyone acting on the candidate's behalf whether they are associated with the campaign or not.

One measure of an ethical campaign would be if the organization has a campaign code of conduct. Certainly, a campaign can be managed ethically without one, but a code of conduct will inform the candidate's strategy and establish clear guidelines for the candidate, staff, and volunteers. Voters can then see if the code is guiding the candidate, even in the heat of the battle when ethical lapses are most likely to occur.

A code of conduct should reflect the core values of the candidate. For example, the code might take into consideration commitment to the public good, honesty, transparency, accountability, integrity, and fairness. The code should establish what kind of campaign conduct comports with these identified values. The code of conduct should make it clear that it applies to anyone involved in the campaign.

To get an idea of what codes can entail, it is helpful to look at a few campaign ethics codes enacted by state legislatures to serve as guides. California, for example, has a voluntary Code of Fair Campaign Practices that is given to all candidates when they file to run for office. California Election Code §20440 provides, in pertinent part:

CALIFORNIA CODE OF FAIR CAMPAIGN PRACTICES
There are basic principles of decency, honesty, and fair play which every candidate for public office in the State of California has a moral obligation to observe and uphold in order that, after vigorously contested but fairly conducted campaigns, our citizens may exercise their constitutional right to a free and untrammeled choice and the will of the people may be fully and clearly expressed on the issues.

THEREFORE:

(1) I SHALL CONDUCT my campaign openly and publicly, discussing the issues as I see them, presenting my record and policies with sincerity and frankness, and criticizing without fear or favor the record and policies of my opponents or political parties that merit this criticism.

(2) I SHALL NOT USE OR PERMIT the use of character defamation, whispering campaigns, libel, slander, or scurrilous attacks on any candidate or his or her personal or family life.

(3) I SHALL NOT USE OR PERMIT any appeal to negative prejudice based on a candidate's actual or perceived race, religious creed, color, national origin, ancestry, physical disability, mental disability, medical condition, marital status, age, sexual orientation, sex, including gender identity, or any other characteristic set forth in Section 12940 of the Government Code, or association with another person who has any of the actual or perceived characteristics set forth in Section 12940 of the Government Code.

(4) I SHALL NOT USE OR PERMIT any dishonest or unethical practice that tends to corrupt or undermine our American system of free elections, or that hampers or prevents the full and free expression of the will of the voters including acts intended to hinder or prevent any eligible person from registering to vote, enrolling to vote, or voting.

(5) I SHALL NOT coerce election help or campaign contributions for myself or for any other candidate from my employees.

(6) I SHALL IMMEDIATELY AND PUBLICLY REPUDIATE support deriving from any individual or group that resorts, on behalf of my candidacy or in opposition to that of my opponent, to the methods and tactics that I condemn. I shall accept responsibility to take firm action against any subordinate who violates any provision of this code or the laws governing elections.

(7) I SHALL DEFEND AND UPHOLD the right of every qualified American voter to full and equal participation in the electoral process.

I, the undersigned, candidate for election to public office in the State of California or treasurer or chairperson of a committee making any independent expenditures, hereby voluntarily endorse, subscribe to, and solemnly pledge myself to conduct my campaign in accordance with the above principles and practices."[56]

Many states, counties, and cities have adopted similar campaign fairness pledges for candidates. Nearly all components of these state and local pledges are voluntary.

Campaign codes often provide a place for the candidate to sign. When you are assessing the ethics of a candidate it is helpful to find out not only whether the candidate has signed a code of conduct, but also whether all staff and volunteers have committed to run an ethical campaign. A good indicator of a candidate's commitment to ethics is whether they make sure that all associated with the campaign are educated about the candidate's values and vision for how the campaign should be run.

Ethical campaigns often have one person who is designated as the de facto ethics officer. Note that this is a separate individual from campaign legal counsel. The ethics officer is a staffer or associate who is prepared to act as an advisor to the candidate when ethical dilemmas arise. The ethics officer is generally responsible for vetting all communications issued by the campaign to ensure they comport with the campaign's values. If a communication is negative, the ethics officer should confirm with campaign staff that the topic is true, fair, and relevant and that there is documentation supporting the allegations. If the campaign communication creates a deceptive inference, it is up to the ethics officer to advise against it. The ethics officer will also oversee actions of consultants, staff, and volunteers to ensure compliance with the code of conduct and should have authority to recommend consequences arising as a result of a violation of the code.

There are many rules and regulations governing campaigns including campaign finance, report filing, signature gathering, advertising content, and signage. These rules are often complicated and provide traps for the unwary. It's not unusual for unscrupulous opponents to anonymously file ethics complaints so that the headlines scream, "Ethics Complaint Filed Against [Candidate X]!" Even if the accused candidate is exonerated, the damage is often done just by virtue of the fact that a complaint has been filed.[57]

Knowing that ethics claims can be used as a weapon in a political campaign–note that the appearance of unethical behavior is a problem–you may want to research the filed complaint to determine whether the existence of the complaint is relevant to your voting decision. Determine who filed the complaint. What was their motive? Was it an honest mistake due to the complexity of the laws, or was it an egregious ethical violation?

Finally, does the candidate demonstrate an honest commitment to ethics? Does his or her announcement speech emphasize the candidate's commitment to running an ethical campaign? Does the candidate publicize a commitment to ethics both on the campaign website and in public interviews? Does the candidate post a signed campaign code of conduct on the campaign website? Has the candidate taken a course on government and/or campaign ethics? When the candidate debates, do they provide respectful and substantive responses to debate questions? Do the actions and behavior of a candidate demonstrate ethical awareness?

When asked by the press to comment negatively about an opponent, does the candidate refuse the bait if the topic is not true, fair, or relevant to the race? Does the candidate try to steer the conversations with the press back to the true issues in the race? Does the candidate challenge the opponent to run an ethical campaign? Does the candidate seem sincerely interested in raising the level of political discourse? Does the candidate have the ability to disagree without being disagreeable?

Finally, does the campaign have a culture that supports safety for staff, volunteers, and consultants? Does the campaign take seriously the threats to data security (including cybersecurity) and have measures in place that strengthen data security and integrity? And does the candidate and his or her campaign promote transparency through its communications, campaign events, and use of artificial intelligence?

When voters are able to determine answers to many of these questions, then they will know if an ethical culture is operating in a candidate's campaign. Having such knowledge allows voters to cast their ballots for ethics!

TAKEAWAYS

Here are five things to look for in assessing the ethical culture of the campaign organization:

1. *Does the candidate set the ethical tone at the top of the organization?*

2. *Does the campaign have a written code of conduct signed by the candidate, staff, and volunteers?*

3. *Does the campaign have a designated ethics officer?*

4. *Has the campaign retained professional counsel on campaign ethics laws?*

5. *Does the candidate demonstrate a commitment to ethical campaigning?*

CHAPTER 5

A PRACTICE OF ETHICAL LEADERSHIP

Ten soldiers wisely led will beat a hundred without a head.

EURIPIDES

If you've read to this point, you have most of the tools you need to assess the leadership practices of a candidate for elected office. Many of this publication's previous chapters touch on leadership fundamentals that can be applied from the Practice of Ethical Leadership[58], a model that explores ways leaders reinforce ethical leadership across all sectors.

Leadership ethics is the study of ethical issues and dilemmas faced by people in leadership roles. It includes who we vote for in elections, since leadership ethics is about issues of leadership and followership.

Ethical leadership is doing the right thing as a leader. How does one determine what is the "right thing" for a leader to do at a certain point in time? First, there is a leader's character to consider. Second, there are specific actions people in formal leadership positions can take to promote ethical behavior in others and respond to situations where things have gone wrong. A leader's character *and* their actions combine to create the impact they can have in their role.

The Candidate as a Role Model

For many voters, a fundamental material element in deciding to vote for someone centers on the candidate's character. While this may appear to be less true in recent election cycles, this publication begins by asking the reader to consider whether or not the candidate takes the high road. That is the heart of the "character question."

> *Leaders spend most of their time learning how to do their work and helping other people learn how to do theirs, yet in the end, it is the quality and character of the leader that determine the performance and results.*
>
> FRANCES HESSELBEIN

We have seen leaders with tremendous expertise and years of experience in elected office plagued by questions of integrity and character that ultimately undermine their ability to accomplish lofty goals. We have also seen leaders with sterling reputations, frequently referred to as being a "good guy," but without experience or expertise to excel in leadership roles.

We want the candidate with both the ability to be a role model and to accomplish great things. There are those who suggest, however, that one should focus on character over competence, since skills can be taught, but integrity and trustworthiness tend to be ideals a person holds and represents or does not. Following the same truism that one should hire for character, so voters, too, should place significant weight on this aspect when considering candidates for elected offices.

It's often noted that power corrupts people. Thus, one can expect that public office holders face a significant test of moral character since elected positions carry with them significant powers of the office. These are valid reasons to consider character the cornerstone of a person's candidacy for elected office.

The Candidate as a Community Builder

In chapter 4, we explored the hallmarks of ethical campaign organizational cultures. To help leaders consider what they can do to foster healthy culture[59], we suggest they focus on building a community of supported relationships. We know that individuals thrive when they are part of such relationships. The steps leaders take to create healthy cultures inevitably lead to organizations that function in ways that respect all aspects of the organization, where the people working in them think about their work in positive ways. The strongest cultures are integrated ones, where people work collaboratively together. How well a campaign functions indicates how well the candidate can lead people with different roles and expertise. It is one proxy for the candidate's ability to build and maintain healthy communities.

What can the voter look for to know if the candidate places a priority on building healthy communities? First, the candidate should have a clear message around what they want to accomplish in office. Think of this as a corollary to an organization's mission or vision: what does this person want to accomplish as an elected official? Earlier, we explored the nature of the candidate's communications and the promises made. These are both good barometers of the worthiness of the candidate's goals. Voters should listen for cues that the candidate wants to serve the office and not the other way around.

Voters should look for evidence that candidates are committed to building strong communities. People especially adept at community building can identify various stakeholders, forge agreements between them, and remain committed to those agreements over time.

Candidates who bring their personal stories to the campaign trail to signal their values, their goals, and their personal practices help to forge relationships between the candidate and the constituency they hope to lead and signal openness –a willingness to be known – that is critical in establishing authentic relationships.

The Candidate Encourages Ethical Conduct
People serving in formal leadership roles accept responsibility for proactively creating an environment of trust within an organization and between an organization and its constituents. Candidates demonstrate their commitment to moral behavior by encouraging moral behavior.

There are certain activities that leaders can undertake to encourage ethical conduct. They can build moral awareness, recognizing when a situation raises ethical issues by identifying them and naming them as such. Often, people especially skilled in this way reframe issues to bring ethical considerations to the forefront. They practice moral decision-making, explicitly taking care and time to determine which course of action is ethically sound. They demonstrate moral intent, identifying which values are taking priority as they make decisions. And they act morally by following through on ethical decisions.

Look for a candidate who demonstrates an understanding of these powerful, explicit acts, but also one who understands that we are all human and that, sometimes, being human gets in the way of moral, ethical behavior. This pragmatic understanding means that a candidate is more likely to support conditions in their campaign and managing themselves that will prevent moral missteps. For example, people are more likely to make ethical lapses when they are tired and physically compromised. Does the candidate take reasonable care of themself and promote a practice of doing so in their campaign?

Another blind spot to ethical conduct is moral fading – failing to recognize when an issue or decision is an ethical one and allowing it to be recast as a business or political decision. Look for candidates who invite others to challenge their thinking and are comfortable walking through their decision-making processes. Many of us make judgments using our intuition rather than our reasoning. Though this works well for many people, it also may allow biases we have to be exploited. A candidate who reverses themself because they have paused to reason or received new information is a sign of a candidate with disciplined decision-making and personal courage. They are willing to accept correction or new information causing them to change their mind or position. And they are tough enough to handle the criticism.

The Candidate Plays Their Position
At the heart of an ethical leadership practice is the leader's commitment to representing the correct interests as called for by the position, or office, one holds. A modern-day sports analogy works well for capturing the essence of this objective. In the leadership model we've developed, we refer to this as playing one's position.[60]

For officeholders, this is one of the clearest distinctions the model offers. Elected officials take oaths as they enter office and those oaths lay out with precision the interests the official is committing to uphold. Sometimes these oaths even make clear an order of preference of various interests that must be supported by the officeholder.

In modern-day politics, a great challenge to this simple principle comes from the system developed in the United States and other countries to advance candidates toward election, the political party system. Originally envisioned as a means to an end, in some people's minds party affiliation has become an end itself. We have countless examples where elected officials continue to pursue loyalty to party at the expense of the interests they have vowed to uphold when entering office. This weakens a system built on serving these oaths, such as democracies. Voters contribute to this problem when they demand absolute fealty to points of view advanced during elections and push the person who is now in office to place promises made on the campaign trail above the interests outlined in the oath of office.

The challenges faced in office often appear quite different once a candidate is now the officeholder. They now have additional information, a new perspective, and growing expertise. This shift is examined in a report prepared by a business CEO, Katherine Gehl, and an academic strategist, Michael Porter, "Why competition in the politics industry is failing America: A strategy for reinvigorating our democracy."[61] In the report, the two apply a model Porter developed as a professor at Harvard Business School to the political party system, which they analyze as an industry. They conclude that the parties are committed to their continuing existence more than they are committed to producing candidates who will uphold oaths of office. The report identifies the problems this creates and some recommended remedies. Candidates take an oath of office, not an oath of party.

When Things Go Wrong, the Candidate Acts to Clarify
We learn a lot about people by how they respond in adverse circumstances. For candidates, this can be when they make a mistake, misspeak on the campaign trail, or when someone in their campaign organization falters. These moments offer leaders a chance for a "do over," if you will, a chance to correct errors or reset expectations among staff and followers.

Since leadership ethics explores the ethical dilemmas faced by leaders and followers, these moments when an error has been made become critical moments in followership. What should you look for in your candidate? The leaders with strong ethical practices will lean on the original vision or purpose they have laid out for their candidacy and accept responsibility for what has happened.

Moving forward, they will make clear the behaviors they will not tolerate on behalf of their candidacy.

This is an opportunity to clarify the culture of the campaign, to reset the priorities and values the candidate is running on, signaling to those working on the campaign and following it what the candidate themself stands for. The candidate might continue to support certain goals but eschew specific tactics to reach those goals, if the tactics do not meet the standards they have set for the campaign. Followers should listen for some evidence of self-reflection and learning on the part of the candidate and a clear explanation for what will be different going forward. Suggestions that others outside the campaign are to be blamed, or that opponents forced the candidate's hand to act this way, may be signs that the candidate is not completely comfortable with the leadership position they are seeking.

The Candidate Contributes to Improving the System
It is a rare leader who can, in addition to fulfilling the obligations of their role, contribute to improving the ecosystem in which the role exists. For business leaders this might look like addressing systemic issues in employment, such as improving pay equality and developing more inclusive work environments. For the elected official, this is someone who has the capacity to contribute to addressing necessary changes in the political system.

This is very different from introducing legislation or regulation aimed at meeting commitments on the campaign trail. Often those most effective at systemic reform have experience in the position and have developed reputations for commitment to the process of politics more than to the goals of a political party. Sometimes, the leader capable of effecting this kind of change is willing to personally sacrifice in a way that has political cost to their constituents to serve a larger purpose of reform. In the political realm, this is often someone who can identify the common good and show followers why they should also be committed to it.

If a candidate is running for office for the first time and does not have a track record that offers voters insight into this capacity for redesigning complex systems, it can be difficult to evaluate the candidate's potential in this area. Past performance in other roles; rhetoric that offers a future, improved vision; and sacrifice of personal goals in favor of common goals are things that voters can look and listen for to evaluate potential leadership capacity in an individual.

The Impact of a Strong Ethical Leadership Practice

The power of each voter's contribution to an election outcome is one of the most compelling attributes of healthy democracies. Armed with information to assess the ethical leadership practice of any candidate, a voter has a method for assessing the potential impact of that candidate once they reach office.

Think of the model as one of cumulative effect, which a visual aid on the website of the Markkula Center for Applied Ethics[62] reinforces. Character is the cornerstone of the model. If the candidate suffers from weak moral character, all actions that person takes will be undermined by the doubt those weaknesses represent in followers' minds. Conversely, if the candidate has a strong character, this provides confidence to followers.

Not all candidates will be equally strong in various actions that can be taken to sustain ethical leadership: creating community, encouraging ethical conduct, playing one's position, clarifying culture, and designing healthier systems. Candidates who can contribute in these areas have the greatest potential for impact. This is the benefit the follower, or voter, can work to assess. Combined with the candidate's character, these abilities point to achievements this candidate can contribute to once in office.

We've heard voters identify weaknesses in candidates and then acknowledge that it is a weakness they also share. This can sound like making the statement, "Well, I'm not any good at that either, but that's why I'm not running for office." Within this self-reflection is the notion that those of us with flaws should not run. We should not be looking for perfect people to hold office, however, because they don't exist. We should be looking for people who want to serve the office they seek, to uphold the commitments they make, rather than people seeking to gain power for their own personal satisfaction or interests. In this way, the voter's character and actions contribute to the political process in much the same way as the candidates', and the practice of ethical leadership can offer as much to the person voting as it can to the person seeking office.

TAKEAWAYS
Here are five hallmarks of ethical leadership to look for in political candidates:

1. *Does the candidate have strong moral character and act with integrity?*

2. *Is the candidate able to create and build community?*

3. *Does the candidate encourage ethical conduct?*

4. *Does the candidate place the interests of the public above all other interests?*

5. *When things go wrong, does the candidate act quickly to accept responsibility and change course where appropriate?*

CHAPTER 6

ARTIFICIAL INTELLIGENCE IN THE ETHICAL CAMPAIGN

What has struck me and has been really remarkable is that the conversation around AI has remained very bipartisan.

ANNA MAKANJU, OpenAI's vice president of global affairs

Both parties hate it.

SAM ALTMAN, CEO, OpenAI[63]

For the 2024 campaign, the introduction of artificial intelligence (AI) and its impact looms large. While dirty tricks in political campaigning may be nothing new, the use of this new technology is and it may only serve to amplify practices that exemplify the underbelly of the American political process without careful planning and intentionality around its use by campaigns. The rules of the road for AI in politics have yet to be written, leaving voters and candidates in this election cycle in a particularly precarious position. The implication for voters is significant: the norms of use for AI will be formed, to a great extent, in the 2024 campaign. Voters should recognize the power they have to influence what will become acceptable behavior by candidates and campaigns going forward, based on how voters respond to candidates' choices now.

On the one hand, there is an expectation among some parts of the electorate that candidates should be up-to-date on the latest technological advancements. Some people running for office may, therefore, feel compelled to demonstrate that they are AI-savvy by using AI in their campaigns. On the other hand, the reputational risks of using AI are significant since the technology's application in elections is unproven and early examples that have gained publicity are, unfortunately, evidence that AI can be used to deploy dirty tricks with more deceit than ever.

To prepare for the increased use of artificial intelligence in campaigns, voters must recognize and reinforce best AI practices from candidates and their campaigns; recognize the role both traditional and social media play in fact-checking and reporting the use of AI; and develop their own best practices to sift through the sea of information and misinformation that has become the hallmark of each campaign election cycle. They must refresh their understanding of cognitive biases; foster critical thinking to analyze the materials that will be used by candidates, PACs, and outside influencers, including people in other countries; and develop information literacy. AI may change elections to such a degree that voters become activists, committed to educating other voters about the implications of AI in elections.

The Backdrop For the 2024 Election
ChatGPT, a commercialized AI chatbot available in both free and premium formats, was launched by OpenAI on November 30, 2022,[64] and it opened a floodgate of AI models made available for general consumption. The excitement about AI's abilities and concerns about its impact and limitations garnered constant media

attention throughout 2023 as candidates prepared and began campaigning for 2024 elections. The 2024 election is not the first where AI will be used, but it is the first where enough low-cost AI tools exist that the potential for it to be incorporated into a number of election-related activities is real.

Though fascinated by chatbots' abilities to write original text and create new illustrations from typed prompts, consumers also learned about some of the challenges AI presents. The models do not always return correct answers, were largely built by being trained on copyrighted material without permission, and have been found to have significant bias built into the systems. Some people raised such concerns about the existential risk to the human race that AI posed that a moratorium on its use was called for in March 2023 and signed by over 33,000 people.[65]

This emerging technology arrived at a time of significant low trust in leaders overall and government leaders in particular. According to the 2023 Edelman Trust Barometer, government leaders are not only distrusted, they were the least trusted institutional leaders in that year's survey.[66] Further, the Barometer identified the United States as one of six countries that are severely polarized.[67] Respondents who identified their countries as severely polarized responded affirmatively to this statement, "I see deep divisions, and I don't think we'll ever get past them."[68]

In identifying the forces that contributed to this polarization, Edelman named one of four forces the "The Battle for Truth," observing media are not trusted either, with "especially low trust in social media."[69]

In the face of these findings, it will be critical for candidates and the press to use AI in ways that increase trust in government and the press, not diminish it. And it will be incumbent on voters to prepare for a campaign cycle using AI.

Into this low trust environment, enter "Ashley," an artificial intelligence campaign volunteer developed by Civox, a London-based company. She is an advanced kind of robocaller candidates can choose to deploy, one who uses no canned or pre-recorded responses and who is capable of having multiple one-on-one, customized conversations with multiple potential voters at the same time.[70] Ashley is fluent in over 20 languages and seen as a way to give underdogs a leg up, equipping them with a better way to understand voters, as Ashley can analyze voters' profiles to tailor conversations to them.[71]

Candidates who choose to use Ashley may feel it is worth the risks, as the tool gives them ways to understand voters better, reach out in different languages, and have longer "conversations" with prospective voters. But what if one of those longer conversations takes an unfortunate turn and Ashley responds in a way inconsistent with the candidate's own beliefs or messages?

Candidates have long had to determine ways to screen and hire campaign workers with integrity, who will campaign in ways that are pre-approved by a campaign manager. Yet there are, sadly, many instances where campaign workers have behaved in ways that damage a candidate's efforts. With human campaign workers, candidates have the option to dismiss the worker and clarify for voters that the worker was acting in a way inconsistent with the campaign's values and culture. (This will only be possible, of course, if the candidate has invested in developing an ethical campaign culture, as described in chapter 4.)

But when a non-human AI system, such as Ashley, behaves badly, who will be accountable for that misstep? Though the person in a campaign who selected the system or made the choice to deploy it can still be held accountable, in these early days of publicly accessible AI we are seeing people held to a higher standard for machine-based mistakes.⁷² AI missteps will reflect badly on candidates both in how the mistake might veer from the campaign's espoused values and the candidate's campaign messages, but also in the fact that the candidate's campaign has had an AI blunder. Voters can use such instances to assess which candidates understand the technology and know how to use it responsibly.

Aside from these ethical dilemmas Ashley presents, there is also the fact that her creators at Civox only intend to sell her to Democratic candidates⁷³, a practice that may draw criticism for being unfair.

Automated AI robocallers aren't the only probable AI applications in the coming election. Already in 2023, the Republican National Committee (RNC) launched an <u>AI-generated video</u> depicting a view of the future if President Biden was re-elected.⁷⁴ Though it was labeled with the words "built entirely with AI imagery" in the upper left-hand corner of the screen, it was so small that users could watch the entire video without noticing it. The video put forth an imagined dystopian version of the future if President Biden is reelected. It relied on exaggeration and AI generated imagery to make its claims.

We will discuss how voters and candidates can prepare for an election rife with synthetic media and the use of chatbots and fundraising systems powered by AI. But it seems the technology companies that built these AI systems anticipated some of the challenges their use would present.

OpenAI restricts any "scaled" use of its products for political purposes so that, for example, using its AI to send out mass personalized emails is not permitted.⁷⁵ However, as noted, AI systems don't always perform as they should, and it seems some of OpenAI's model performance in the political realm is not consistent with the company's statements.

DALL-E is an image generation AI system developed by OpenAI. OpenAI prohibits DALL-E from creating public figures, and when Reuters tried to create images of former President Trump or President Biden, the request was blocked with a message that said doing so "may not follow our content policy."[76] However, the Reuters reporters were able to create images of other politicians,[77] demonstrating how challenged AI creators are by creating fair and safe use conditions for their products.

This moment does not arrive without some guardrails in the form of existing campaign regulation. One such regulation, relevant to the use of AI in elections, is regulation 110.16 from the Federal Election Commission.[78] It reads:

§110.16 Prohibitions on fraudulent misrepresentations.

a. *In general.*
   No person who is a candidate for Federal office or an employee or agent of such a candidate shall—
   1. Fraudulently misrepresent the person or any committee or organization under the person's control as speaking or writing or otherwise acting for or on behalf of any other candidate or political party or employee or agent thereof in a matter which is damaging to such other candidate or political party or employee or agent thereof; or
   2. Willfully and knowingly participate in or conspire to participate in any plan, scheme, or design to violate paragraph (a)(1) of this section.

b. *Fraudulent solicitation of funds.*
   No person shall—
   1. Fraudulently misrepresent the person as speaking, writing, or otherwise acting for or on behalf of any candidate

or political party or employee or agent thereof for the purpose of soliciting contributions or donations; or
2. Willfully and knowingly participate in or conspire to participate in any plan, scheme, or design to violate paragraph (b)(1) of this section.

In this way, some of the potential for "deepfakes"—AI created images or sounds falsely representing people running for office—which includes a candidate and their opponents, is mitigated. They are not permitted. The FEC is considering making the language in this regulation more explicit regarding artificial intelligence and invited public comment about this proposed change in the Fall of 2023.[79] The National Conference of State Legislatures tracks statewide current statutes that may also apply to the use of AI in elections, as well as legislation passed in 2023 specific to its use in elections.[80]

The concern, of course, is that deceptive artificial intelligence in campaign ads will occur on a scale that will make policing their use challenging, if not impossible. This is where the voting public comes in. We turn now to the best practices for candidates, the press, and voters, in preparation for elections in the age of AI.

Best Practices for Campaigns, Media, and Voters in the Age of AI

A fundamental question campaigns should be able to address, and voters should ask of candidates, is, "How does the use of AI by the candidate protect or advance the voters' interests?" Publicly elected officials should always be asking if an action they take or a decision they make serves the voters' interests, and the use of artificial intelligence is no exception. AI that is used, for example, to bring forward greater clarity around issues or provide more transparency in data by helping to analyze it are uses of AI that align with voters' interests. Ethical campaigns will ask themselves if the application of AI they are considering helps voters and steer away from those uses that do not.

For this reason, voters should be on the lookout for a policy statement from candidates explaining when and why AI is being used in their campaign. It is a best practice to disclose the use of AI in circumstances when it is interacting with the public, but also when it is being used in internal campaign operations.

Earlier in the book, we discussed the fact that it is a rare leader who can contribute to improving the political campaign ecosystem, and it is hard to evaluate a candidate's capacity in this realm if they have never held office before. What is the corollary to ethical system design when it comes to AI?

Officials elected in the 2024 election cycle will have many ways to influence the adoption of AI in our society, given that it is a relatively new technology being developed in a nascent industry. Candidates should expect questions about their position on AI safety, trustworthiness, and fairness as they run for office. They will have a unique opportunity to demonstrate their capacity in designing ethical systems as they consider what incentives should be created and limitations placed on the development and deployment of AI systems. Voters should look for candidates with well-developed points of view about AI. If the candidate does not possess expertise in this area, the voter should look to see that the candidate has aligned with others who have expertise in AI.

And candidates will need to be sure their positions on regulation of AI align with their practices on the campaign trail. Someone supporting watermarking—the practice of marking AI systems in a way that makes it evident to users that an AI system is being deployed—should, for example, consistently mark campaign materials created and activities supported by the use of AI whether they are images in brochures or fundraising databases. Or, if they are taking a stand on the fact that AI systems should not be trained on copyrighted materials, they might want to consider using Firefly for any image generation their campaign does. This model, developed by Adobe, was trained using only materials that are Adobe stock images, openly licensed content, or public domain content.[81]

One concern about AI use has to do with bias in AI systems, often baked into models due to the materials used to train the system because materials developed by humans have inherent biases within them. But new resources are emerging that can help campaigns, and the voters holding them accountable, to know how AI models stack up when it comes to bias.

Common Sense Media is a nonprofit organization that reviews media and technology and provides ratings that parents can use to determine the appropriateness of certain media for their children given their age. It is developing a rating system for AI systems. Though there are only relatively few reviews as of January 2024 and the reviews are written with children in mind, they do provide commentary on bias and other ethical harms and risks in the models reviewed.

The review for Stable Diffusion notes, among other things, that the model was only intended for research use, even though it is free and available to the public.[82] Their website quotes from Stable Diffusion's model card that, "while the capabilities of the image generation models are impressive, they can also reinforce or exacerbate social biases." Common Sense Media also notes that these warnings do not appear on the sites where Stable Diffusion can be downloaded.

These are only a few of the value-laden decisions to consider around the use of AI. There are systems that give the user ownership over any prompts and outputs and those that don't, just to offer up one more consideration. We offer these examples not by way of endorsing or discouraging the use of any of these AI systems by individuals acting in their own interests. But we hope the landmines that exist for candidates around the use of AI are becoming easier to spot.

What's the takeaway for candidates? That AI is a complex technology and few people fully grasp how the models are built and what their best use cases are. Candidates will want to be sure their campaigns are researching AI choices carefully and that they can explain those choices to people who inquire about them. Voters will want to explore both candidates' views on this new technology from a policy perspective, but also see how those policy statements align with the choices each campaign is making about technology deployment.

Voters need to deploy their best critical thinking skills to navigate technology's impact on election cycles from social media to artificial intelligence. Gathering evidence, applying logic and reasoning to analysis provided by others, and talking with others over the issues that surface in an election are all ways that voters can prepare to vote responsibly.

As noted already, artificial intelligence is fundamentally biased because it is trained on sets of data that may be incomplete or rife with human biases. Just knowing about biases is not enough to combat them. It's a bias, in fact, to think that it is. This is known as the GI Joe fallacy after a popular TV cartoon in the 1980s that used to end with a saying, "Now you know. And knowing is half the battle."[83] Scholars writing about this phenomenon point out, "The real power of online behavioral control comes not from knowledge, but from things like situation selection, habit formation, and emotion regulation."[84] In other words, we can't rely on our own understanding that there is bias in the world to protect us from our own. We need to use tools and plan for ways to mitigate those biases.

During elections, for example, we can decide to proactively seek information about candidates and issues rather than relying only on the information that comes to us via our mailboxes, inboxes, and social media platforms. When information comes to us, we can check its sources, take note of who has funded its distribution and look for obvious signs of the use of artificial intelligence to make images,[85] such as slick visuals, hands missing fingers, earrings or ears that don't match, or random artifacts placed in odd areas.[86] We can decide not to query AI systems with prompts asking for information about candidates, since we know such systems do not reliably return accurate information and are trained using biased datasets.

All of these actions contribute to developing information literacy, which, along with critical thinking, is a powerful skill set for voters to develop. Voters should be thinking about:

- the source of the information they are consuming,

- how it was gathered,

- what the process was for vetting or editing it, and

- how it is being reported or shared.[87]

Sources that have decades-long reputations for providing credible information to voters, such as the League of Women Voters (lwv.org), are great primary sources. Tools that voters can use include fact-checking sites such as Factcheck.org, PolitiFact, which we have already mentioned, Snopes, and The Fact Checker.[88] There are also resources to help voters know more about an image's authenticity. Google has a reverse image search at images.google.com, as do websites such as TinEye.com.[89]

Voters should also familiarize themselves with the news sources reporting best practices in the age of artificial intelligence. Our colleague at the Markkula Center, Subbu Vincent, has provided some practical guidance to reporters covering political ads that offers insights for voters, as well. These are some of the questions Vincent recommends that reporters ask before reporting about an ad, and they can also guide voters about what to consider when consuming media:

1. "Who released the ad? Is the ad about a candidate the ad's sponsor supports, or does it contain messages against or attacking an opponent? If the ad is from the candidate's side and contains falsehoods or lies about the candidate, the FEC can look into it. If the ad implicates an opponent, and lies or falsehoods about them, the FEC has no leeway.
2. Is it satire? For instance, The Daily Show did a satirical generative AI video on President Biden[90], which is easy to tell because of their branding on the visual. The Lincoln Project added a laugh track to a video former President Trump posted about the indictments and the January 6th committee.[91]
3. If it's not satire, the review demands go higher. Identify where generative AI was used. Video, audio, text, headline, mix of all of these? Did the producer disclose that?
4. Dig around and ascertain whether the public figure in the ad actually said those things somewhere in speech. Details matter.
5. Even if they said it, that does not make the claim itself true or false automatically. A review of the claim or claims (also called fact-checking) is going to be needed. Or if it was already fact-checked, those results – such as true, false, partially true, etc. – would already be available from major fact-checking organizations or peer news sites.

6. Is the ad simply using generative AI to create the likeness of a person to relay an otherwise true or factual message? The newsroom needs to know if the producers are trying to cut costs by generating the candidate's likeness instead of recording a conventional new video with them. That leads to the question of whether the candidate authorized the likeness.
7. Likewise, is the ad simply using generative AI to create the likeness of a person to relay a rhetorical claim, and hence is not fact-checkable because it is too general? Such claims are protected political speech anyway. For example, Donald Trump may have never actually said, 'Biden miserably messed up in handling Maui,' but a generative AI ad could simply use Trump's likeness to show him saying that." In which case, did he authorize that rendition?"[92]

Vincent also recommends stronger labeling of AI-generated political ads, describing an example where an ad attacking Ron DeSantis was labeled "Generative AI Political Ad".[93] Vincent suggests that news outlets could go even one step further and offers this example: "The advertisement contains generated audio, using text posted by the person X or Y on platform Z. Person X did not say this."[94]

It is helpful for voters to know these recommendations so they can view political advertising through this lens and ask themselves if reporters have addressed these issues in their reporting on political advertising to account for the potential use of artificial intelligence in those ads.

The use of AI in elections is relatively uncharted territory. To prepare for the experience, voters should recognize the best practices for using AI and evaluate candidates and their campaigns on their ability to follow them; understand the role that the press plays in fact-checking and reporting the use of AI; and develop personal information literacy practices.

TAKEAWAYS

Here are five things to look for in preparation for the use of artificial intelligence in elections:

1. *Do you understand the potential harm AI can have in eroding trust further by misleading or confusing voters by using AI in deceptive ways?*

2. *Are there labels or other indications that AI has been used in political advertising?*

3. *Do candidates have a policy statement on their use of AI in their campaigns?*

4. *Do candidates' positions on AI policy matters reconcile with their own uses of AI?*

5. *Have you developed information literacy practices to help you assess the source and nature of election information you are using, including the use of time-tested, trustworthy sources for political information?*

CHAPTER 7

ETHICAL CANDIDATES SUPPORT THE RULE OF LAW

A republic, if you can keep it ...

BENJAMIN FRANKLIN[95]

Ethical candidates—and public officials—must state that they will abide by the Constitution and the certified outcomes of elections for all offices. Such a pledge from candidates serves the public interest and the common good.[96] But it also projects several ethical virtues[97] that we believe are necessary in candidates: honesty, integrity, and transparency. Voters must know where candidates stand on basic elements of ethical conduct and the broader commitment to following the rule of law.

A commitment to honoring one's duty to honor the rule of law might seem unnecessary to some. After all, aren't candidates for office and those serving in elected positions committed—both legally and morally—to abiding by the Constitution, laws, and election procedures? It would be reasonable to conclude that this would be the case in a democracy. But that assumption was rocked in the 2020 presidential election, and the country is still dealing with what happened and why.

The 2020 presidential election opened the eyes of voters to an otherwise unthinkable set of events in U.S. politics. That is, witnessing an incumbent president seeking reelection, claiming that the election had been stolen from him, and refusing to concede the office or welcome the newly elected president. And then it got worse.

On January 6, 2021, the day on which the Congress would formally convene to review and officially record the tally of votes from the Electoral College, the incumbent president, following weeks of denying that he had lost the election, urged his supporters to march on the Capitol and stop Congress from certifying the Electoral College results.[98] What followed was a violent attack to take over control of Congress, including calls for violence against the Vice President and Congressional leaders who were doing their constitutional duty to follow the rule of law and certify the election results.[99] The attack on the Capitol and public officials was an insurrection, "a violent uprising against an authority or government."[100]

How could such things happen in a 230-year-old Democracy? What happened to the ethical duty to serve the rule of law and the moral imperative of promoting the public interest and the common good for which our Democratic Republic was created by the founders? We learned much from the U.S. House of Representatives' investigation of the January 6 insurrection.[101] From planning the effort to stop the certification of the Electoral College vote to supercharging the political climate with false claims of a stolen election, multiple actors sought to stop the peaceful transition of power and thwart the will of the voters. In order to understand the importance of loyalty to the rule of law, we believe it is important to know what happened in the lead-up to the 2020 election and in the weeks and months that followed.

What Happened After the November 2020 Elections?
Many individuals played a part in the historically-unprecedented political events that developed following the election of Joseph R. Biden as the 46th president in 2020. Here is a brief rundown on unethical developments that followed Biden's win in November 2020:

1. Donald Trump, the incumbent president and a candidate for reelection, and his campaign officials claimed that the election had been stolen from him. This set in motion a number of efforts to "stop the steal."[102]
2. Claims of a stolen election spread widely from statements by Trump and national Republican Party leaders and elected officials, and by the Trump campaign. This would become known as "The Big Lie."[103]
3. Social media became a platform for the spread of lies about the legitimacy of Biden's election and an organizing medium for efforts to interfere with the transition of power.[104]
4. Trump, his campaign officials and lawyers, and Republican public officials undertook a national effort to challenge the certified outcomes of state and local election officials, threatened election officials, and filed dozens of baseless lawsuits to overturn election results in several states. Trump refused to concede the election.[105]
5. Elected representatives in Congress and in state legislatures called for actions to change election laws and voting rights, all under the false claim that we needed to restore integrity to election results.[106]
6. When most of the above efforts failed to achieve their goals, Trump and his loyalists publicly called for a movement to come to Washington, D.C., and stop the peaceful transition of the presidency. They promoted a national effort to deny the legitimacy of Biden's election.[107]

7. A violent attack on the Capitol took place on January 6, 2021, during which several people died and many police officers were injured.[108]
8. Ultimately, Joseph Biden was confirmed as president, and he was sworn in on January 20, 2021.
9. Many political leaders and candidates continue to deny the lawful election of President Biden, years after the election was certified.[109]
10. At the beginning of 2024, about one third of Americans continued to believe that Biden is not the legitimate president due to a stolen election, a view held by a majority of Republicans.[110]

Supporting the U.S. Constitution and the Constitutions of the States

We can learn a great deal from the events that followed the 2020 presidential election. Perhaps the most important one is that candidates and public officials must abide by the Constitution and the constitutions of the 50 states. These documents are the ultimate codification of the rule of law, and citizens have an ethical duty to follow such.

The 2020 presidential election has been described by government agencies and independent researchers as the "most secure election in American history."[111] This was due in part to responses to threats that arose during the 2016 presidential election when there were attempts to compromise electoral systems by foreign and domestic actors, often using cyberattacks on state and local election administration.[112]

During the period of November 6, 2020 to January 20, 2021, many candidates, elected public officials, and national political leaders refused to abide by the rules that define how elections are to be conducted, certified, and supported by winners and losers. Many tried to prevent the transition of power to the newly elected president, which threatened the centuries-long duty of loyalty to the rule of law. To this day, many public officials maintain that President Biden was not legitimately elected and have continued to spread "election denialism" in our political environment.[113]

Why is it important to become informed of candidates and their actions and positions on issues? Those that are elected to serve in public office will have anywhere from two to six years in office to impact our democratic system of government. Voters who are better informed on candidates and their positions are better able to cast their ballots for those who will bring ethical behavior to their roles in government. If those with less ethical perspectives or intentions are elected to office, then in most cases citizens must live with their choices until the next election cycle. Harm to the body politic by unethical officials can be detrimental to trust in government and could result in undermining the legitimacy of our system of government. Being informed and choosing wisely—voting for ethics—is important to good government.

State Legislatures and Efforts to Restrict Voting
An alarming development in the wake of the 2020 election has been the concerted efforts of legislators and other public officials in many states to restrict voting rights rather than protect and expand voting in this country. Arguing that restrictions on voting are needed to "restore integrity" to the electoral process, many state legislators and other public officials have used the debunked claims of a stolen election and massive voter fraud to justify their proposals for new laws to restrict voting rights. What do these look like?

Well, in the wake of the 2020 election and what followed, a concerted and organized effort began in many states to change voting rights and access to the balloting process. According to the Brennan Center for Justice's *Election Integrity* project,[114] beginning in 2021 440 bills were introduced in 49 states to restrict voting in some way. Of these bills, we witnessed 34 adopted in 19 states.[115] Similarly, in 2022, a midterm and state elections year, at least 408 restrictive bills were considered by lawmakers in 39 states. We saw 11 restrictive voting laws adopted in eight states.[116]

As 2023 ended, over 350 bills were introduced in 47 state legislatures that were intended to restrict or suppress voting. Of these, 14 states added new restrictive laws in that year.[117] If one looks at the totality of state legislative restrictions on voting since the 2020 election, nearly 1,200 bills were introduced in state legislatures and about 59 became law between 2021-2023. Although the number of new laws enacted to restrict voting rights or the processes of voting was a small portion of the bills that were introduced, the organized efforts of state legislators to enact restrictions on people's rights when it came to voting was unprecedented and an unfortunate effort to curtail voting rights.

The new *restrictive* laws that were adopted include:[118]

- ☐ Making it more difficult to register to vote
- ☐ Requiring stricter voter identification for registered voters
- ☐ Restricting when voting can take place, often limiting early voting, mail-in ballots, or times of day for casting ballots
- ☐ Limiting where polling places can be established, often reducing the number of polling locations, closing polling on college campuses, or forcing many voters to travel farther and wait longer to cast a ballot
- ☐ Limiting drop-off boxes for mail or absentee ballots

An ethical candidate or public official would not support restricting voting rights, but instead would promote easy access to

the ballot and encourage the widest voter turnout possible. Laws and procedures that *expand* voting rights would include such processes as:
- ☐ Same-day voter registration and voting
- ☐ Absentee voting for all without an excuse
- ☐ Early voting times and convenient locations
- ☐ Provisional voting for those whose credentials are challenged
- ☐ All-mail voting
- ☐ Convenient overseas and military voting options

Expanding and promoting the right to vote is the ethical path to elections in a democracy. In 2023, more than 50 bills were adopted into law in 23 states that expanded or promoted voting.[119]

Candidates who favor expanding voting often demonstrate the ethical standards of citizens' rights and fairness.[120] Candidates and public officials who seek to restrict voting are demonstrating unethical behavior and lacking the ethical virtues that are expected of those who aspire to government service. Even if a legislative body can approve new laws that restrict voting and that are legally recognized upon adoption, it does not mean that these new laws are ethical. Voters should look for candidates who are committed to voting rights and seek to expand and preserve these rights for voters in their states. Ethical candidates are more likely to be ethical public officials.

Efforts to Interfere with State and Local Election Authorities

With a large swath of the population believing that there was vote fraud leading to a stolen election in 2020, it is not surprising that some state legislatures have sought to "restore integrity" to the voting process by changing the rules under which state and local election authorities have been carrying out their duty to administer, conduct, and certify elections. And according to research by the Brennan Center for Justice,[121] the effort to interfere with election authorities has not been rare. Unlike voting restrictions that are targeted at citizens' ability to participate in elections, election interference is any action that hinders the ability of election officials to do their legally assigned duties. These actions can occur before, during, or after voters have cast their ballots.

In the two years that followed the 2020 election, we witnessed seven states enacting about a dozen election interference laws, following the introduction of more than 150 bills across 27 states.[122] As of the end of 2023, of more than 80 bills introduced in at least 23 states, seven laws were adopted in six states to hinder the administration of elections or to subvert the legitimate outcomes of elections.[123] From 2021 to 2023, nearly 250 bills were introduced at the state level to interfere with the normal duties of election officials.

Examples of unethical laws or procedures that *interfere* with or subvert the election process have been growing in several states, and include:[124]

- ☐ Allowing state legislators to control election results
- ☐ Invalidating actions by duly-appointed election authorities
- ☐ Permitting poll watchers to interfere with balloting
- ☐ Restricting assistance to voters
- ☐ Partisan interference in election tabulation and certification
- ☐ Intimidation of election volunteers and officials

Voters must look at who supported these bills and laws and understand the ethical implications of these actions. State and local election officials take an oath to uphold the constitution and the rule of law in overseeing the administration and certification of elections within their jurisdiction. When laws are adopted that allow for partisan interests to subvert the legitimate work of state and local election authorities, we witness the failure of one's ethical duties to protect rights, demonstrate fairness, and promote the common good.

More appropriately, state and local election laws and processes should seek to ensure fair and honest elections. Election integrity is enhanced by procedures that protect election processes, respect local election authorities, and provide security to the balloting process and to the volunteers who serve as election judges and workers. This would include *election integrity* procedures such as:[125]

- ☐ Assigning effective administrative powers to state and local election authorities
- ☐ Providing reasonable and factual assistance to voters at polling places
- ☐ Managing voter registration rolls in a professional, nonpartisan fashion
- ☐ Protecting the safety and security of polling officials and volunteers
- ☐ Barring legislative officials from interfering in the certification of elections or overturning actions of local election authorities
- ☐ Implementing secure voting systems with broad and deep cybersecurity

It is important to know where candidates stand on matters of voting rights[126] and fair and honest elections. Expanding voting rights and protecting the integrity of election administration and certification are ethical duties of public officials. Candidates for office who will not support these goals or who seek to restrict voting and voting rights or interfere in the process of conducting and certifying elections are unethical and should not be elected to hold public office.

An Ethical Assessment of Voter Restrictions and Interference in Election Outcomes

The Framework for Ethical Decision Making[127] can illuminate a path toward a better assessment of the positions of candidates from a series of ethical lenses. The framework employs six possible lenses for examining a potential decision: rights, fairness and justice, virtue, the common good, utilitarianism, and care.[128] Let's review several of these key ethical standards or lenses that can be used by voters to evaluate candidates for office:

The Rights Lens

In many ways, there can be no more essential right in a democracy than the right to vote. This is a constitutional right that has been expanded over 230 years through amendments that extended voting rights to blacks, women, and younger voters. Federal statutory enforcement of the right to vote has helped to protect voters and includes landmark legislation such as the Voting Rights Act of 1965 and its renewals.[129]

Applying the rights lens to making a decision about a candidate might examine the following:

- ☐ Policies that support the Rights Lens: Promoting voter registration and early voting options.
- ☐ Policies that fail the Rights Lens: Limiting the use of mail ballots or unwarranted purging of voter rolls prior to an election.

The Fairness and Justice Lens

Individuals should be treated the same, unless they differ in ways that are relevant to the situation in which they are involved. Unfortunately, some voting rules have included unfair and unjust practices that restricted voting by persons of color for much of our history, including such examples as Jim Crow laws, literacy tests, and suppression of voting.

Applying the lens of fairness and justice to making a decision about a candidate could result in the following example findings:

- ☐ Policies that support Fairness and Justice Lens: Permitting the casting of a provisional ballot, an option when a voter's registration cannot be validated at the polling place.
- ☐ Policies that fail on the Fairness and Justice Lens: Reducing polling locations and hours for casting ballots.

The Virtue Lens

Facts matter and the truth is essential for trust. Nearly every state and local election official has a deep commitment to the integrity of the electoral processes that have been entrusted to their administration. Many electoral processes and rules are a product of honesty, integrity, and honor to the rule of law. But if a law or rule does not promote integrity in elections, it lacks important ethical virtues.

Applying the Virtue Lens to making a decision about a candidate could result in the following example findings:

- ☐ Policies that support the Virtue Lens: Protecting professional election authorities and election security.
- ☐ Policies that lack virtue: Encouraging the intimidation of election workers.

The Common Good Lens

Governments have a special duty to act impartially and to serve the common good. What does this mean? "The common good, then, consists primarily of having the social systems, institutions, and environments on which we all depend work in a manner that benefits all people."[130] Fundamentally, the right to vote promotes the common good in a democracy. Public officials and candidates for office should act to promote the public interest—not a partisan one. Laws for elections and voting should be adopted if they will benefit the common good of society. Election laws should secure greater benefits for the common good.

Applying the Common Good lens to making a decision about a candidate could result in the following example findings:

- ☐ Policies that support the Common Good: All-mail voting and a period of early voting.
- ☐ Policies that fail the Common Good: Subverting election administration to overturn legitimate outcomes.

Applying the Framework for Ethical Decision Making to examine the actions of candidates and public officials offers a way for voters to assess the ethics underlying candidate positions and officials' actions in regard to voting and election laws and policies.

Why the Rule of Law Matters in a Democracy
No democracy can survive if public officials are willing to ignore the rule of law. Candidates who choose to run for public office should demonstrate in their words and actions that they have and will support the rule of law as elected public officials. To elect individuals to public office who promote actions to subvert federal or state constitutions, laws, and the rule of law, is to place democracy in jeopardy.

Voters have an ethical duty to be informed about candidates and their positions on support for the rule of law and emerging issues. By being an informed voter, citizens can help to ensure that ethical candidates will be elected and that the future of a democracy based upon the rule of law is secure.

TAKEAWAYS

Here are five things to look for when evaluating the commitment of candidates to honor the rule of law:

1. *Does the candidate state in their speeches and campaign materials that they support the rule of law, including the Constitution and election laws?*

2. *Does the candidate support legislation and laws that expand voting rights?*

3. *Has the candidate supported efforts to expand voting or voting rights?*

4. *Does the candidate support the legitimate administration of elections by state and local election officials?*

5. *Does the candidate agree to accept the certified results of an election and support a peaceful transition of power to the winner of the election?*

CHAPTER 8

WHAT YOU CAN DO TO ENCOURAGE ETHICAL CAMPAIGNS

Public sentiment is everything. With public sentiment nothing can fail; without it nothing can succeed.

ABRAHAM LINCOLN

At this point, you may be asking yourself, "What am I to do?" The previous chapters have outlined the ethical characteristics to look for in candidates and political campaigns. So, why should you join a movement to bring about more ethics in political campaigns? Will it make a difference or has this country lost the battle to bring an ethical culture to its campaigns and elections? Though the path to an ethical campaign culture is not beyond our grasp, there is an incline to climb first.

According to a poll conducted by Georgetown University's Institute of Politics and Public Service in 2023,[131] voters remain pessimistic about the chances of resolving some of the political divisions that characterize U.S. politics. However, the poll also found that voters want more respect and civility to bridge the partisan divide and voters want "…'a politician who is willing to work together to get things done, even if it means compromising on my values sometimes' (67%) over 'a politician who consistently fights for my values, even if this means not finding a solution very often'

(31%)." Since politicians sadly don't seem to be willing to seek a respectful approach to campaigns that will foster what is best for the public interest, it is up to us to send them a message that we want them to conduct civil and ethical campaigns. Here are a few suggestions on how you can do just that.

Publicize Your Commitment to Ethics in Political Campaigns

Contact campaigns in your area and let the candidates know that so long as you agree with the candidate's policies, you are planning on casting your vote for the candidate who runs the most ethical campaign. Most campaign websites have a contact form where you can provide comments such as these to the candidate. This sounds simple, but we believe this kind of proactive outreach can be very effective.

Write letters to the editor of your local paper telling them of your commitment to ethical campaigning. In your letter let your neighbors and the candidate know that all things being equal, you will be voting for the candidate you deem most ethical at the end of the campaign. Use your social media platforms to share your objectives and commitment to supporting ethical candidates during upcoming elections.

Create a Campaign Ethics Report Card

Another suggestion is to grade candidates on their ethics and send them a report card. The report card would evaluate the candidates on a scale from one to ten, with ten being the most ethical. The total amount would represent the candidate's campaign ethics score. The higher the score, the more ethical the candidate.

At the beginning of the campaign, share the report card criteria with candidates and alert them to the fact that they will be graded. In your letter to the editor described above, you can also share your intent to grade the candidates. The completed report card would then be sent to the candidate and the press a month before Election Day, as early voting begins.

We suggest that candidates be evaluated on the following criteria:

CANDIDATE ETHICS REPORT CARD

- Is the candidate respectful to their opponent and refuses to engage in mudslinging?

- Does the candidate have a code of conduct for their campaign?

- Does the candidate discourage dirty tricks or any unfair campaign practices?

- Are the candidate's ads and other assertions true, fair, and relevant?

- Does the candidate stick to the issues and provide substantive information about their policy positions?

- Is the candidate willing to debate their opponent(s)?

- Does the candidate refrain from using public resources for political purposes?

- Is the candidate a good steward of campaign funds?

- Does the candidate build community, encourage ethical conduct in their campaign, and put the public's interest before their own? If there are missteps, does the candidate move quickly and appropriately to resolve them?

- Does the candidate use AI responsibly in the campaign?

- Is the candidate committed to the rule of law and supporting the certified outcome of elections?

Ask Others to Encourage Ethical Campaigning

Wouldn't it be great to start a campaign ethics movement? One way to get the ball rolling is to enlist your friends and associates on social media. Explain your interest in improving the campaign process. Share your campaign ethics scorecard and suggest that they too grade the candidates on their campaign ethics.

If you are associated with any endorsing groups, you might want to ask them to include questions about campaign ethics in the candidate questionnaires. For example, the candidate can be asked about whether they have a code of conduct in place for their campaign. Or the candidate might be asked what their strategy is for responding to political attacks.

You can also reach out to newspaper editorial boards and ask them to include questions about campaign ethics in their endorsement interviews.

Contact well-regarded government groups, such as the League of Women Voters, and share with them your ethical scorecard template so their members can also judge candidates on their ethics.

You may want to contact the local leadership of the political party with which you are affiliated and ask the party to include campaign ethics as part of their party platform.

Consider contacting organizations that are sponsoring debates and asking them to include questions about campaign ethics in the debate questions.

Encourage Ethical Political Debates

Political debates, particularly for presidential races, often leave us begging for more. The sound bites and zingers tossed around on the debate stage give us very little information about what a candidate stands for or how they will react in any given situation. Based on the premise that our political process is born out of the ethical ideal of creating an informed electorate, the Markkula Center for Applied Ethics has developed the following 15 suggestions for debates:

Improving the Political Debate Process

- Candidates must pledge to participate in the debates.

- Candidates should agree to Rules of Ethical Debate Engagement (see below) before being granted permission to debate.

- Eliminate the live audience except in town hall-style debate formats. (This will help to eliminate the circus atmosphere, discourage grandstanding, and allow more time to be devoted to candidate responses.)

- There should be more debates, with smaller groups of candidates. (This will help eliminate the yelling from the candidates on the ends trying to get recognized.)

- The debates should be more conversational and less confrontational, perhaps with moderators and candidates sitting around a table.

- Each debate should focus on a few specific topics.

- Candidates should be given the opportunity to respond if their policy or record is attacked.

- All participants should be allotted the same amount of speaking time.

- Time limits should allow for thoughtful and complete answers, not sound bites.

- Assuming candidates are allowed sufficient time to respond to the moderator or fellow candidate(s), microphones should be turned off if a candidate exceeds the allotted time.

- If, after three warnings, a candidate continues to violate debate time or conduct rules, the candidate's stage lighting should be turned off for the duration of the debate.

- Debates should be taped with a two-hour delay for broadcast, so fact-checking can be accomplished and displayed at the same time television audiences are viewing the debate. (This may be difficult to implement in a world in which we are accustomed to live political events and instant comments online from viewers, but it is hoped that this will result in more honest exchanges on the debate stage.)

- Moderators should ask questions that identify both (a) widely endorsed public goals and (b) how those goals compete with each other in certain policy questions, asking the candidate to explain how they would prioritize or balance those goals in their proposed policy. (This would identify and compare the various trade-offs included in each candidate's proposals.)

- There should be hypothetical questions which will reveal the principles that inform a candidate's decision-making. (Let's find out what makes them tick.)

- Moderators should not ask candidates to raise hands to support or oppose a position without opportunity for follow-up, because such questions suggest the framework for the question is set and simplistic.

The Markkula Center for Applied Ethics has also developed the following rules of ethical debate engagement that, if followed, will help inform voters.

The Markkula Rules of Ethical Debate Engagement

Candidates should show respect for the electorate:

- ☐ They should provide substantive answers to the moderator's questions.
- ☐ They should be honest, fair, and civil in all their responses.
- ☐ They should only make promises that are consistent, capable of being achieved, and within the jurisdiction of the office being sought.

Candidates should show respect for their opponents:

- ☐ They should criticize policies and the record of their opponents, not the opponents personally.
- ☐ They should refrain from name-calling or other insults.
- ☐ They should not engage in irrelevant attacks against either their opponents or their opponents' family or associates.

Candidates should show respect for the debate process:

- ☐ They should not interrupt or shout down fellow candidates or the moderator.
- ☐ They should answer the question asked.
- ☐ They should stay within allotted time limits.
- ☐ They should use their time to debate opponents and not to make soundbites for publicity.

You may wish to contact the debate sponsoring organizations and ask that they require candidates to operate under these rules of engagement. Ask candidates to agree to these standards of debate conduct—and request that they demand that their opponents do so, as well.

Vote for Ethics

If you have followed the above suggestions, you have told the candidates that you want them to conduct civil and ethical campaigns. You have warned them that you will be grading their campaign based on criteria provided to them. And you have followed their campaign conduct and evaluated their ethics.

Election Day is the day to show the candidates that you mean it. If one candidate stands out as the more ethical campaigner – and, of course, if you agree with their policies – then by all means, vote for that candidate, which will be a vote for Ethics!

TAKEAWAYS

Here are five things you can do to encourage ethical campaigns:

1. *Publicize your commitment to ethics in political campaigns*

2. *Create a campaign ethics scorecard*

3. *Start an ethical campaign movement by enlisting others*

4. *Encourage debate sponsors to adopt rules of ethical debate engagement*

5. *Vote for ethics!*

CONCLUSION

The course of history is directed by the choices we make, and our choices grow out of the ideas, the beliefs, the values, the dreams of the people.

ELEANOR ROOSEVELT

Ethical conduct in political campaigns, as in other human endeavors, requires information, preparation, and personal reflection. With the overarching goal of strengthening democracy, ethical candidates engage in campaign practices that will inform the electorate, restore trust in government, and fulfill ethical duties owed to us, the people the candidate seeks to represent. Candidates who establish early on a set of principles and ethical guidelines for their campaign will help inform their decision-making when confronted with the ethical choices all candidates face in the course of a political race.

Never forget that political candidates are, in essence, applying for a job, and we the voters are their future employers. The job that they seek is a position of trust: we, as future constituents, should be able to trust them to be a good steward of public funds, trust them to always act on our behalf, trust them to uphold the rule of law, and trust them to always act in the public's best interest, not their own. When candidates enter public service, they will assume fiduciary duties of loyalty, care, and fairness as a result of the trust we have placed in them. In order to get the job, a candidate's campaign should demonstrate that they understand these duties and that the candidate is committed to working for the common good. Political campaigns are often the first time, and sometimes the only way, the public learns about would-be elected officials. If a candidate campaigns with integrity, they will send a clear signal to us as to how the candidate will govern. Campaigning is an undertaking to demonstrate that candidates possess ethical awareness and would bring that trait to public service.

To borrow from John Adams, imagine a political world where "greatness, not meanness" is the norm, where people trust their elected officials, and where public service is once again considered a noble calling. By dedicating yourself to increasing ethical behavior in political campaigns, you have taken the first step in helping make that vision a reality. So, let's start that ethical campaign movement. Let's tell the world that we *vote for ethics*.

ENDNOTES

1   Donna Brazile, "Russian DNC Narrative Played Out Exactly As They Hoped," *Time,* March 17, 2017, http://time.com/4705515/donna-brazile-russia-emails-clinton/

2   Katie Reilly, "Read Hillary Clinton's 'Basket of Deplorables' Remarks About Donald Trump Supporters," *Time,* September 10, 2016, http://time.com/4486502/hillary-clinton-basket-of-deplorables-transcript/

3   Nolan D. McCaskill, "Trump Accuses Cruz's Father of Helping JFK Assassin," *Politico,* May 3, 2016, https://www.politico.com/blogs/2016-gop-primary-live-updates-and-results/2016/05/trump-ted-cruz-father-222730

4   Derek Hawkins, "No, You Can't Text Your Vote. But These Fake Ads Tell Clinton Supporters to Do Just That," *Washington Post,* November 3, 2016, https://www.washingtonpost.com/news/morning-mix/wp/2016/11/03/no-you-cant-text-your-vote-but-these-ads-tell-clinton-supporters-to-do-just-that/?utm_term=.f8f57a9121f4

5   Ryan Lizza, "Ted Cruz's Iowa Mailers Are More Fraudulent than Everyone Thinks," *The New Yorker,* January 31, 2016, https://www.newyorker.com/news/news-desk/ted-cruzs-iowa-mailers-are-more-fraudulent-than-everyone-thinks

6   Alexandra Jaffe, "Donald Trump Has 'Small Hands,' Marco Rubio Says," *NBC News*, February 29, 2016, https://www.nbcnews.com/politics/2016-election/donald-trump-has-small-hands-marco-rubio-says-n527791

7   Steve Eder and Jonathan Martin, "Videos Put Democrats on Defensive About Dirty Tricks," *New York Times*, October 20, 2016, https://www.nytimes.com/2016/10/21/us/politics/video-dnc-trump-rallies.html

8   Jenna Johnson, "Timeline of Donald Trump and Ted Cruz Bickering About Their Wives," *Washington Post*, March 24, 2016, https://www.washingtonpost.com/news/post-politics/wp/2016/03/24/timeline-of-donald-trump-and-ted-cruz-bickering-about-their-wives/?utm_term=.3f414a66c38c

9   Robert S. Mueller, III, *Report on the Investigation into Russian Interference in the 2016 Presidential Election*, (U.S. Department of Justice, March 2019), https://apps.npr.org/documents/document.html?id=5955997-Muellerreport

10   Ben Kamisar, "Almost a third of Americans still believe the 2020 election result was fraudulent," *NBC News*, June 20, 2023, https://www.nbcnews.com/meet-the-press/meetthepress-blog/almost-third-americans-still-believe-2020-election-result-was-fraudule-rcna90145

11   Kamisar, "Almost a third of Americans still believe the 2020 election result was fraudulent."

12   "Trust in Government," *Gallup*, 2024, https://news.gallup.com/poll/5392/trust-government.aspx

13	United States Election Project, "2016 November General Election Turnout Rates," United States Election Project Website, Electproject.org, http://www.electproject.org/2016g

14	"Voter turnout, 2018-2022," *Pew Research Center*, July 12, 2023, https://www.pewresearch.org/politics/2023/07/12/voter-turnout-2018-2022/

15	Drew Desilver, "Turnout in U.S. has soared in recent elections but by some measures still trails that of many other countries," *Pew Research Center*, November 1, 2022, https://www.pewresearch.org/short-reads/2022/11/01/turnout-in-u-s-has-soared-in-recent-elections-but-by-some-measures-still-trails-that-of-many-other-countries/

16	Christine Trost and Matt Grossmann, eds., *Win the Right Way: How to Run Effective Local Campaigns in California* (Berkeley: Berkeley Public Policy Press, Institute of Governmental Studies, 2005)

17	Letter from John Adams to James Warren, 22 April 1776, *National Archives: Founders Online*, https://founders.archives.gov/documents/Adams/06-04-02-0052

18	Joseph Cummins, *Anything for a Vote: Dirty Tricks, Cheap Shots, and October Surprises in U.S. Presidential Campaigns* (Philadelphia: Quirk Books, 2015), Kindle Edition.

19	Cummins, *Anything for a Vote: Dirty Tricks, Cheap Shots, and October Surprises in U.S. Presidential Campaigns*

20	Richard Nixon Foundation, "Watergate Explained," June 2022, https://www.nixonfoundation.org/watergate-explained/;

see also, Michael Koncewicz, "How Republican dirty tricks paved the way for Russian meddling in 2016," *The Washington Post*, March 9, 2018, https://www.washingtonpost.com/news/made-by-history/wp/2018/03/09/how-republican-dirty-tricks-paved-the-way-for-russian-meddling-in-2016/

21   Bob Greene, "Mudslinging Campaigns Hurt the Country," CNN, September 2, 2012, http://www.cnn.com/2012/09/02/opinion/greene-campaign-mud-slinging/index.html

22   Lydia Saad, "Trump and Clinton Finish with Historically Poor Images," Gallup Poll, November 8, 2016, https://news.gallup.com/poll/197231/trump-clinton-finish-historically-poor-images.aspx

23   Jonathan Martin and Alexander Burns, "With Cross Talk, Lies and Mockery, Trump Tramples Decorum in Debate with Biden," *New York Times*, Sept. 29, 2020, https://www.nytimes.com/2020/09/29/us/politics/trump-biden-debate.html

24   Jeffrey M. Jones, "Record Low in U.S. Satisfied With Way Democracy Is Working," *Gallup*, January 5, 2024, https://news.gallup.com/poll/548120/record-low-satisfied-democracy-working.aspx

25   Joe Guzzardi, "Goldwater Refused to Exploit a Sex Scandal Involving Top LBJ Assistant," *Lodi News-Sentinel*, August 31, 2007, https://www.lodinews.com/opinion/columnists/joe_guzzardi/article_7b3adeaf-ccb4-5d0f-a0ce-24de05e-9adc7.html

26   Katharine Q. Seelye, "The 2000 Campaign: The Debate; Gore Aide Receives, Then Lets Go of Hot Potato," *New York Times*, September 14, 2000, https://www.nytimes.com/2000/09/14/us/the-2000-campaign-the-debate-gore-aide-receives-then-lets-go-of-hot-potato.html

27   Jonathan Martin and Amie Parnes, "McCain: Obama Not an Arab, Crowd Boos," *Politico*, October 10, 2008, https://www.politico.com/story/2008/10/mccain-obama-not-an-arab-crowd-boos-014479

28   "Read Barack Obama's Eulogy of John McCain," *New York Times*, September 1, 2018, https://www.nytimes.com/2018/09/01/us/politics/barack-obama-john-mccain-funeral-eulogy.html

29   Commission on Presidential Debates, "October 21, 1984, debate transcript," *Commission on Presidential Debates website, Debates.org*, October 21, 1984, http://www.debates.org/index.php?page=october-21-1984-debate-transcript

30   Robin Abcarian, "Michelle Obama's Stunning Convention Speech: 'When They Go Low, We Go High,'" *Los Angeles Times*, July 25, 2016 http://www.latimes.com/politics/la-na-pol-michelle-speech-20160725-snap-story.html

31   Pranshu Verma and Gerrit De Vynck, "AI is destabilizing 'the concept of truth itself' in 2024 election," *The Washington Post,* January 22, 2024, https://www.washingtonpost.com/technology/2024/01/22/ai-deepfake-elections-politicians/

32 American Association of Political Consultants, "AAPC Board of Directors' Declaration Regarding 'Push Polling,'" *The American Association of Political Consultants Website, TheAAPC.org,* https://theaapc.org/about-us/policy-statements-2/push-polling-statement/

33 See Sander Van Der Linden, "AI-Generated Fake News Is Coming to an Election Near You," *Wired,* January 22, 2024, https://www.wired.com/story/ai-generated-fake-news-is-coming-to-an-election-near-you/#:~:text=AI%20has%20effectively%20democratized%20the,fake%20news%20stories%20in%20minutes; and Zeve Sanderson, Solomon Messing, and Joshua A. Tucker, "Misunderstood mechanics: How AI, TikTok, and the liar's dividend might affect the 2024 elections," *Brookings,* January 22, 2024, https://www.brookings.edu/articles/misunderstood-mechanics-how-ai-tiktok-and-the-liars-dividend-might-affect-the-2024-elections/

34 Dana Radcliffe, "The Cost of Deceptive Politics," *Huffington Post,* November 9, 2012 (updated January 9, 2013), https://www.huffingtonpost.com/dana-radcliffe/political-lies_b_2094820.html

35 For a list of reputable fact checkers, see: University of California-Berkeley Library, "Real News/Fake News: Fact Checkers," November 27, 2023, https://guides.lib.berkeley.edu/fake-news

36 Zachary B. Wolf, "The 5 key elements of Trump's Big Lie and how it came to be," *CNN,* May 19, 2021, https://www.cnn.com/2021/05/19/politics/donald-trump-big-lie-explainer/index.html

37   Jennifer Agiesta and Ariel Edwards-Levy, "CNN Poll: Percentage of Republicans who think Biden's 2020 win was illegitimate ticks back up near 70%," *CNN*, August 3, 2023, https://www.cnn.com/2023/08/03/politics/cnn-poll-republicans-think-2020-election-illegitimate/index.html

38   See Subramaniam Vincent, "How Social Media Has Harmed the Growth of Democratic Culture by Design," March 9, 2021, https://www.scu.edu/ethics/all-about-ethics/how-social-media-has-harmed-the-growth-of-democratic-culture-by-design/

39   Federal Election Commission, "Citizens United v. FEC," https://www.fec.gov/legal-resources/court-cases/citizens-united-v-fec/

40   Native Advertising Institute, "Native Advertising Defined," *Native Advertising Institute Website, NativeAdvertisingInstitute.org*, https://nativeadvertisinginstitute.com/resources/native-advertising-definition/

41   L. Sandy Maisel, "Candidates: Promises and Persuasion," in *Shades of Gray: Perspectives on Campaign Ethics*, eds. Candace J. Nelson, David A. Dulio, and Stephen K. Medvik (Washington, D.C.: Brookings Institution Press, 2002), 55

42   Maisel, "Candidates, Promises and Persuasion," 55

43   See Hana Callaghan, *Voting for Ethics*, 2020, Chapter 2, p. 28.

44   Amy Howe, "Justice Stevens Goes to the Senate," *SCOTUS Blog, May 1, 2014, https://www.scotusblog.com/2014/05/justice-stevens-goes-to-the-senate/*

45   See generally, Lawrence Lessig, *Republic, Lost: How Money Corrupts Congress—and a Plan to Stop It* (New York: Twelve, Hatchette Book Group, 2011)

46   *See* Lessig, *Republic, Lost*

47   Hana Callaghan, "Public Officials as Fiduciaries," Markkula Center for Applied Ethics, May 31, 2016, https://www.scu.edu/government-ethics/resources/public-officials-as-fiduciaries/

48   Federal Election Commission, "Making independent expenditures," https://www.fec.gov/help-candidates-and-committees/making-independent-expenditures/

49   "Independent expenditure," *Ballotpedia*, https://ballotpedia.org/Independent_expenditure

50   Nonprofits organized under Internal Revenue Code Section 501(c)(4) or 501(c)(6) do not have to disclose members. For more information *see,* https://www.opensecrets.org/outsidespending/nonprof_summ.php

51   Callaghan, "Public Officials as Fiduciaries."

52   Institute for Local Government, "Campaigning for Re-election: Legal and Ethical Red Flags," *Institute for Local Government Website, CA-ILG.org*, August, 2010; updated April, 2014, http://www.ca-ilg.org/sites/main/files/file-attachments/7-red_flags_august_2014_update.pdf

53   Nik Popli, "What We Learned from the Scathing Ethics Report on George Santos," *Time,* November 16, 2023, https://time.com/6336275/george-santos-ethics-report/

54   Michael S. Schmidt, "Lavish Lifestyle of a Lawmaker Yields Federal Charges," *New York Times,* February 15, 2013, http://www.nytimes.com/2013/02/16/us/politics/jesse-jackson-jr-charged-in-misuse-of-campaign-money.html

55   California Fair Political Practices Commission, "Information for State Candidates, Their Controlled Committees, and Primarily Formed Committees for State Candidates," California Fair Political Practices Commission Website, FPPC.org, August, 2018, Manual 1, Chapter 6, http://www.fppc.ca.gov/content/dam/fppc/NS-Documents/TAD/Campaign%20Manuals/Manual_1/Entire-Manual-1.pdf

56   See Casetext, "California election code §20440," https://casetext.com/statute/california-codes/california-elections-code/division-20-election-campaigns/chapter-5-fair-campaign-practices/article-3-code-of-fair-campaign-practices/section-20440-providing-blank-form-of-code-and-copy-of-chapter

57   Some examples of ethics complaints filed in the 2024 presidential campaign, include: Jill Colvin and Brendan Farrington, "Trump allies file ethics complaint against Gov. DeSantis," *AP News,* March 15, 2023, https://apnews.com/article/trump-desantis-ethics-complaint-2024-presidential-campaign-e887199fb9f63ef2051295eced5068ce ; and Alex Thompson, "Scoop: Watchdog files FEC complaint against Dean Phillips," *Axios,* January 3, 2024, https://www.axios.com/2024/01/04/dean-phillips-steve-schmidt-super-pac-fec

58   Ann Skeet, "The Practice of Ethical Leadership." The Markkula Center for Applied Ethics at Santa Clara University, April 2017.

59   Ann Skeet, "Defining Healthy Organizational Culture." The Markkula Center for Applied Ethics at Santa Clara University, October 2019.

60   Skeet, "The Practice of Ethical Leadership."

61   Katherine Gehl and Michael Porter, "Why Competition in the Politics Industry is Failing America." Harvard Business School, September 2017 https://www.hbs.edu/competitiveness/Documents/why-competition-in-the-politics-industry-is-failing-america.pdf

62   Ann Skeet, "The Practice of Ethical Leadership" infographic. The Markkula Center for Applied Ethics at Santa Clara University, April 2017.

63   Brad Stone, "AI Leaders Contemplate a Big Election Year," *Bloomberg,* January 17, 2024, https://www.bloomberg.com/news/newsletters/2024-01-17/davos-2024-sam-altman-and-satya-nadella-talk-ai-and-elections

64   "Introducing ChatGPT," *OpenAI,* November 30, 2022, https://openai.com/blog/chatgpt

65   "Pause Giant AI Experiments: An Open Letter," Future of Life Institute, March 22, 2023, https://futureoflife.org/open-letter/pause-giant-ai-experiments/

66   Edelman Trust Barometer Global Report, *Edelman,* January 15, 2023, page 11, available as of 1/6/24 at https://www.edelman.com/sites/g/files/aatuss191/files/2023-03/2023%20Edelman%20Trust%20Barometer%20Global%20Report%20FINAL.pdf

67   Edelman Trust Barometer Global Report, page 16.

68   Edelman Trust Barometer Global Report, page 15

69   Edelman Trust Barometer Global Report, page 14

70   Anna Tong and Helen Coster, "Meet Ashley, the world's first AI-powered political campaign caller," *Reuters*, December 15, 2023, available as of 1/6/24 at https://www.reuters.com/technology/meet-ashley-worlds-first-ai-powered-political-campaign-caller-2023-12-12

71   Tong and Coster, "Meet Ashley, the world's first AI-powered political campaign caller."

72   Ann Skeet, "ChatGPT has revived interest in ethics. The irony is that we haven't been holding humans to the same standards," *Fortune.com*, January 22, 2024, https://fortune.com/2024/01/22/chatgpt-revived-ethics-human-leadership/

73   Tong and Coster, "Meet Ashley, the world's first AI-powered political campaign caller."

74   Alex Thompson, "First look: RNC slams Biden in AI-generated ad," *Axios,* April 25, 2023, available as of 1/6/24 at https://www.axios.com/2023/04/25/rnc-slams-biden-re-election-bid-ai-generated-ad

75   Alexandra Ulmer and Anna Tong, "Deepfaking it: America's 2024 election collides with AI boom," *Reuters,* May 30, 2023, available as of 1/6/24 at https://www.reuters.com/world/us/deepfaking-it-americas-2024-election-collides-with-ai-boom-2023-05-30/

76   Ulmer and Tong, "Deepfaking it."

77   Ulmer and Tong, "Deepfaking it."

78   Federal Election Commission, United States of America, Regulations, as of 1/6/24 available at https://www.fec.gov/regulations/110-16/2023-annual-110 - 110-16

79   "Comments sought on amending regulation to include deliberately deceptive Artificial Intelligence in campaign ads," Federal Election Commission, August 16, 2023, available as of 1/12/24 at https://www.fec.gov/updates/comments-sought-on-amending-regulation-to-include-deliberately-deceptive-artificial-intelligence-in-campaign-ads/

80   "Artificial Intelligence (AI) in Elections and Campaigns," National Conference of State Legislatures, updated December 7, 2023, https://www.ncsl.org/elections-and-campaigns/artificial-intelligence-ai-in-elections-and-campaigns

81   Adobe Products, Firefly, available as of 1/12/24 at https://www.adobe.com/products/firefly.html

82   Common Sense Media, product review for Stable Diffusion, https://www.commonsensemedia.org/ai-ratings/stable-diffusion

83   Laurie R. Santos and Tamar Gendler, "2014: What Scientific Idea is Ready for Retirement?" *Edge*, https://www.edge.org/response-detail/25436

84   Santos and Gendler, "2014: What Scientific Idea is Ready for Retirement?"

85   Meghan Bartels, "How to Tell If a Photo is an AI-Generated Fake," *Scientific American*, March 31, 2023, https://www.scientificamerican.com/article/how-to-tell-if-a-photo-is-an-ai-generated-fake/

86   Kashmir Hill and Jeremy White, "Designed to Deceive: Do These People Look Real to You?" *New York Times*, November 21, 2020, https://www.nytimes.com/interactive/2020/11/21/science/artificial-intelligence-fake-people-faces.html

87   Developed drawing from private communications and discussions at the Markkula Center for Applied Ethics weekly "Issues" meeting where ethical issues in current events are discussed. Many resources for identifying quality content exist, including this resource from the International Federation of Libraries, https://repository.ifla.org/bitstream/123456789/167/1/How_to_Spot_Fake_News-Full-resolution.jpg

88   Ken Budd, "11 Ways to Fight Election Misinformation," *AARP*, September 13, 2023, https://www.aarp.org/politics-society/government-elections/info-2023/spot-election-misinformation.html

89   Budd, "11 Ways to Fight Election Misinformation."

90   "A.I. Joe Biden is NOT Holding Back in This Ad," The Daily Show, YouTube, available as of January 15, 2024 at https://www.youtube.com/watch?v=JONzK-AUzro

91   The Lincoln Project, social media site X, available as of January 15, 2024 at https://twitter.com/ProjectLincoln/status/1692574681474150473

92   Subramaniam Vincent, "How We Can Protect Against Deceptive AI Political Ads," *Forbes.com*, August 29, 2023.

93   Vincent, "How We Can Protect Against Deceptive AI Political Ads."

94   Vincent, "How We Can Protect Against Deceptive AI Political Ads."

95   Benjamin Franklin's response to Elizabeth Willing Powel, "September 17, 1787: A Republic, If You Can Keep It," *The Constitutional Convention: A Day by Day Account for September 1787.* https://www.nps.gov/articles/000/constitutionalconvention-september17.htm#:~:text=%2D%2DBenjamin%20Franklin's%20response%20to,a%20republic%20or%20a%20monarchy%3F%22

96   Manuel Velasquez, Claire Andre, Thomas Shanks, S.J., and Michael J. Meyer, "The Common Good," Markkula Center for Applied Ethics, August 2, 2014, https://www.scu.edu/ethics/ethics-resources/ethical-decision-making/the-common-good/

97   Manuel Velasquez, Claire Andre, Thomas Shanks, S.J., and Michael J. Meyer, "Ethics and Virtue," Markkula Center for Applied Ethics, January 1, 1988, https://www.scu.edu/ethics/ethics-resources/ethical-decision-making/ethics-and-virtue/

98   Charlie Savage, "Incitement to Riot? What Trump Told Supporters Before Mob Stormed Capitol," *New York Times*, January 10, 2021, https://www.nytimes.com/2021/01/10/us/trump-speech-riot.html

99   Sheera Frenkel, "The storming of Capitol Hill was organized on social media," *New York Times*, January 6, 2021, https://www.nytimes.com/2021/01/06/us/politics/protesters-storm-capitol-hill-building.html

100   A similar definition of an insurrection can be found in many dictionaries and encyclopedias. The definition quoted here is from Oxford Reference, https://www.oxfordreference.com/display/10.1093/oi/authority.20111006213516658#:~:text=insurrectionist%20n.,insurrection%20was%20savagely%20put%20down.

101   House Select Committee to Investigate the January 6th Attack on the United States Capitol, *Final Report: Select Committee to Investigate the January 6th Attack on the United States Capitol*, 117th Congress Second Session, House Report 117-663, December 22, 2022, https://www.govinfo.gov/content/pkg/GPO-J6-REPORT/pdf/GPO-J6-REPORT.pdf

102   Sarah Hansen, "Trump Campaign Paid $3.5 Million To Stop The Steal Organizers, Report Finds," *Forbes*, June 29, 2021, https://www.forbes.com/sites/sarahhansen/2021/02/10/

trump-campaign-paid-35-million-to-stop-the-steal-organizers-report-finds/?sh=993529337ae3

103   Zachary B. Wolf, "The 5 key elements of Trump's Big Lie and how it came to be," *CNN*, May 19, 2021, https://www.cnn.com/2021/05/19/politics/donald-trump-big-lie-explainer/index.html

104   Frenkel, "The storming of Capitol Hill was organized on social media."

105   House Select Committee to Investigate the January 6th Attack on the United States Capitol, "Final Report."

106   See Brennan Center for Justice, "Election Misinformation," https://www.brennancenter.org/election-misinformation ; and Mekela Panditharatne, et al., "Information Gaps and Misinformation in the 2022 Elections," August 2, 2022, https://www.brennancenter.org/our-work/research-reports/information-gaps-and-misinformation-2022-elections

107   See House Select Committee to Investigate the January 6th Attack on the United States Capitol, "Final Report."; and Christian Paz, "Remember Trump's Accomplices," *The Atlantic*, February 18, 2021, https://www.theatlantic.com/ideas/archive/2021/02/remember-republicans-who-betrayed-democracy/617769/

108   House Select Committee to Investigate the January 6th Attack on the United States Capitol, "Final Report."

109   There are many examples of "election deniers" who claim that Joseph Biden did not win the 2020 presidential

election. For example, see: Savannah Kuchar, "'Alive and well': Election deniers linger in statewide, presidential elections," *USA Today*, October 9, 2023, https://www.usatoday.com/story/news/politics/2023/10/09/election-deniers-running-for-office/70903244007/; and States United Democracy Center, "Election Deniers Make Up One-Third of Congress, One Year Out from Congressional Certification of 2024," January 5, 2024, https://statesuniteddemocracy.org/electiondeniers-congress/

110   Jennifer Agiesta and Ariel Edwards-Levy, "CNN Poll: Percentage of Republicans who think Biden's 2020 win was illegitimate ticks back up near 70%," *CNN*, August 3, 2023, https://www.cnn.com/2023/08/03/politics/cnn-poll-republicans-think-2020-election-illegitimate/index.html

111   Election Infrastructure Government Coordinating Council, "Joint Statement from Elections Infrastructure Government Coordinating Council & the Election Infrastructure Sector Coordinating Executive Committees," *U.S. Cybersecurity and Infrastructure Security Agency*, November 12, 2020, https://www.cisa.gov/news-events/news/joint-statement-elections-infrastructure-government-coordinating-council-election

112   David E. Sanger and Catie Edmondson, "Russia Targeted Election Systems in All 50 States, Report Finds," *New York Times*, July 25, 2019, https://www.nytimes.com/2019/07/25/us/politics/russian-hacking-elections.html#:~:text=WASHINGTON%20%E2%80%94%20The%20Senate%20Intelligence%20Committee,federal%20officials%20at%20the%20time; and Christina A. Cassidy, " Lessons learned from 2016, but US faces new election threats," *AP News*, January 26, 2020, https://apnews.com/article/ap-top-news-elections-voting-hillary-clinton-hacking-502ea2d593ed7ae74162c8eb46290b8a

113   Kuchar, "'Alive and well': Election deniers linger in statewide, presidential elections."

114   Brennan Center for Justice, "Election Integrity," https://www.brennancenter.org/issues/defend-our-elections/election-integrity

115   Brennan Center for Justice, "Voting Laws Roundup: December 2021," January 12, 2022, https://www.brennancenter.org/our-work/research-reports/voting-laws-roundup-december-2021

116   Brennan Center for Justice, "Voting Laws Roundup: December 2022," February 1, 2023, https://www.brennancenter.org/our-work/research-reports/voting-laws-roundup-december-2022

117   Brennan Center for Justice, "Voting Laws Roundup: 2023 in Review," January 18, 2024, https://www.brennancenter.org/our-work/research-reports/voting-laws-roundup-2023-review

118   To track new voting laws in the states, see: Brennan Center for Justice, "State Voting Laws," https://www.brennancenter.org/issues/ensure-every-american-can-vote/voting-reform/state-voting-laws

119   Brennan Center for Justice, "Voting Laws Roundup: 2023 in Review."

120   Markkula Center for Applied Ethics, "A framework for ethical decision making," https://www.scu.edu/ethics/ethics-resources/a-framework-for-ethical-decision-making/

121	Brennan Center for Justice, "Election Integrity."

122	Brennan Center for Justice, "Voting Laws Roundup: December 2022."

123	Brennan Center for Justice, "Voting Laws Roundup: 2023 in Review."

124	See Brennan Center for Justice, "Election Integrity."

125	See Brennan Center for Justice, "Voting Laws Roundup: 2023 in Review."

126	League of Women Voters, "Voting Rights," https://www.lwv.org/voting-rights; and Common Cause, "Protecting the Right to Vote," https://www.commoncause.org/our-work/voting-and-elections/voting-rights/?source=adwords&gad_source=1&gclid=Cj0KCQiAwbitBhDIARIsABfFYIL7DiNhEs-yPvF6zvuUCv-0ivXywHenWF1c5wrlL0kJ6gF3OSOtVcLoaAo8kE-ALw_wcB

127	Markkula Center for Applied Ethics, "A framework for ethical decision making."

128	Markkula Center for Applied Ethics, "A framework for ethical decision making."

129	National Archives, "Voting Rights Act (1965)," https://www.archives.gov/milestone-documents/voting-rights-act; Nick Corasaniti, "How the Voting Rights Act, Newly Challenged, Has Long Been Under Attack," *New York Times,* November 21, 2023, https://www.nytimes.com/2023/11/21/us/politics/voting-rights-act-history.html

130   Manuel Velasquez, et al., "The Common Good."

131   "September 2023 Battleground Civility Poll," Institute of Politics and Public Service, Georgetown University, September 20, 2023, https://politics.georgetown.edu/2023/09/20/september-2023-battleground-civility-poll/

APPENDIX A

A FRAMEWORK FOR ETHICAL DECISION MAKING FROM THE MARKKULA CENTER FOR APPLIED ETHICS[1]

We all have an image of our better selves, of how we are when we act ethically or are "at our best." We probably also have an image of what an ethical community, an ethical business, an ethical government, or an ethical society should be. Ethics really has to do with all these levels—acting ethically as individuals, creating ethical organizations and governments, and making our society as a whole ethical in the way it treats everyone.

WHAT IS ETHICS?

Simply stated, ethics refers to standards of behavior that tell us how human beings ought to act in the many situations in which they find themselves—as friends, parents, children, citizens, businesspeople, teachers, professionals, and so on.

It is helpful to identify what ethics is NOT:

- ☐ **Ethics is not the same as feelings.** Feelings do provide important information for our ethical choices. However, while some people have highly developed habits that make

---

[1] This framework is from the Markkula Center for Applied Ethics and the language is nearly identical to the current framework that has been published before on the center's website. See: Markkula Center for Applied Ethics, "A framework for ethical decision making," November 8, 2021, https://www.scu.edu/ethics/ethics-resources/a-framework-for-ethical-decision-making/

them feel bad when they do something wrong, others feel good even though they are doing something wrong. And, often, our feelings will tell us that it is uncomfortable to do the right thing if it is difficult.

- ☐ **Ethics is not the same as religion.** Many people are not religious but act ethically, and some religious people act unethically. Religious traditions can, however, develop and advocate for high ethical standards, such as the Golden Rule.
- ☐ **Ethics is not the same thing as following the law.** A good system of law does incorporate many ethical standards, but law can deviate from what is ethical. Law can become ethically corrupt—a function of power alone and designed to serve the interests of narrow groups. Law may also have a difficult time designing or enforcing standards in some important areas and may be slow to address new problems.
- ☐ **Ethics is not the same as following culturally accepted norms.** Cultures can include both ethical and unethical customs, expectations, and behaviors. While assessing norms, it is important to recognize how one's ethical views can be limited by one's own cultural perspective or background, alongside being culturally sensitive to others.
- ☐ **Ethics is not science.** Social and natural science can provide important data to help us make better and more informed ethical choices. But science alone does not tell us what we ought to do. Some things may be scientifically or technologically possible and yet unethical to develop and deploy.

Why Identifying Ethical Standards is Hard

There are two fundamental problems in identifying the ethical standards we are to follow:

1. On what do we base our ethical standards?
2. How do those standards get applied to specific situations we face?

If our ethics are not based on feelings, religion, law, accepted social practice, or science, what are they based on? Many philosophers and ethicists have helped us answer this critical question. They have suggested a variety of different lenses that help us perceive ethical dimensions. Here are six of them:

Six Ethical Lenses

The Rights Lens

Some suggest that the ethical action is the one that best protects and respects the moral rights of those affected. This approach starts from the belief that humans have a dignity based on their human nature per se or on their ability to freely choose what they do with their lives. On the basis of such dignity, they have a right to be treated as ends in themselves and not merely as means to other ends. The list of moral rights—including the rights to make one's own choices about what kind of life to lead, to be told the truth, not to be injured, to a degree of privacy, and so on—is widely debated; some argue that non-humans have rights, too. Rights are also often understood as implying duties—in particular, the duty to respect others' rights and dignity.

The Justice Lens

Justice is the idea that each person should be given their due, and what people are due is often interpreted as fair or equal treatment. Equal treatment implies that people should be treated as equals according to some defensible standard such as merit or need, but not necessarily that everyone should be treated in the exact same way in every respect. There are different types of justice that address what people are due in various contexts. These include social justice (structuring the basic institutions of society), distributive justice (distributing benefits and burdens), corrective justice (repairing past injustices), retributive justice (determining how to appropriately punish wrongdoers), and restorative or transformational justice (restoring relationships or transforming social structures as an alternative to criminal punishment).

The Utilitarian Lens

Some ethicists begin by asking, "How will this action impact everyone affected?"—emphasizing the consequences of our actions. Utilitarianism, a results-based approach, says that the ethical action is the one that produces the greatest balance of good over harm for as many stakeholders as possible. It requires an accurate determination of the likelihood of a particular result and its impact. For example, the ethical corporate action, then, is the one that produces the greatest good and does the least harm for all who are affected—customers, employees, shareholders, the community, and the environment. Cost/benefit analysis is another consequentialist approach.

The Common Good Lens

According to the common good approach, life in community is a good in itself and our actions should contribute to that life. This approach suggests that the interlocking relationships of society are the basis of ethical reasoning and that respect and compassion for all others—especially the vulnerable—are requirements of such reasoning. This approach also calls attention to the common conditions that are important to the welfare of everyone—such as clean air and water, a system of laws, effective police and fire departments, health care, a public educational system, or even public recreational areas. Unlike the utilitarian lens, which sums up and aggregates goods for every individual, the common good lens highlights mutual concern for the shared interests of all members of a community.

The Virtue Lens
A very ancient approach to ethics argues that ethical actions ought to be consistent with certain ideal virtues that provide for the full development of our humanity. These virtues are dispositions and habits that enable us to act according to the highest potential of our character and on behalf of values like truth and beauty. Honesty, courage, compassion, generosity, tolerance, love, fidelity, integrity, fairness, self-control, and prudence are all examples of virtues. Virtue ethics asks of any action, "What kind of person will I become if I do this?" or "Is this action consistent with my acting at my best?"

The Care Ethics Lens
Care ethics is rooted in relationships and in the need to listen and respond to individuals in their specific circumstances, rather than merely following rules or calculating utility. It privileges the flourishing of embodied individuals in their relationships and values interdependence, not just independence. It relies on empathy to gain a deep appreciation of the interest, feelings, and viewpoints of each stakeholder, employing care, kindness, compassion, generosity, and a concern for others to resolve ethical conflicts. Care ethics holds that options for resolution must account for the

relationships, concerns, and feelings of all stakeholders. Focusing on connecting intimate interpersonal duties to societal duties, an ethics of care might counsel, for example, a more holistic approach to public health policy that considers food security, transportation access, fair wages, housing support, and environmental protection alongside physical health.

Using the Lenses
Each of the lenses introduced above helps us determine what standards of behavior and character traits can be considered right and good. There are still problems to be solved, however.

The first problem is that we may not agree on the content of some of these specific lenses. For example, we may not all agree on the same set of human and civil rights. We may not agree on what constitutes the common good. We may not even agree on what is a good and what is a harm.

The second problem is that the different lenses may lead to different answers to the question, "What is ethical?" Nonetheless, each one gives us important insights in the process of deciding what is ethical in a particular circumstance.

Making Decisions
Making good ethical decisions requires a trained sensitivity to ethical issues and a practiced method for exploring the ethical aspects of a decision and weighing the considerations that should impact our choice of a course of action. Having a method for ethical decision making is absolutely essential. When practiced regularly, the method becomes so familiar that we work through it automatically without consulting the specific steps.

The more novel and difficult the ethical choice we face, the more we need to rely on discussion and dialogue with others about the dilemma. Only by careful exploration of the problem, aided by the insights and different perspectives of others, can we make good ethical choices in such situations.

We have found the following framework for ethical decision making a useful method for exploring ethical dilemmas and identifying ethical courses of action.

A FRAMEWORK FOR ETHICAL DECISION MAKING

Identify the Ethical Issues
1. Could this decision or situation be damaging to someone or to some group, or unevenly beneficial to people? Does this decision involve a choice between a good and bad alternative, or perhaps between two "goods" or between two "bads"?
2. Is this issue about more than solely what is legal or what is most efficient? If so, how?

Get the Facts
3. What are the relevant facts of the case? What facts are not known? Can I learn more about the situation? Do I know enough to make a decision?
4. What individuals and groups have an important stake in the outcome? Are the concerns of some of those individuals or groups more important? Why?
5. What are the options for acting? Have all the relevant persons and groups been consulted? Have I identified creative options?

Evaluate Alternative Actions

6. Evaluate the options by asking the following questions:

   - ☐ Which option best respects the rights of all who have a stake? (The Rights Lens)
   - ☐ Which option treats people fairly, giving them each what they are due? (The Justice Lens)
   - ☐ Which option will produce the most good and do the least harm for as many stakeholders as possible? (The Utilitarian Lens)
   - ☐ Which option best serves the community as a whole, not just some members? (The Common Good Lens)
   - ☐ Which option leads me to act as the sort of person I want to be? (The Virtue Lens)
   - ☐ Which option appropriately takes into account the relationships, concerns, and feelings of all stakeholders? (The Care Ethics Lens)

Choose an Option for Action and Test It

7. After an evaluation using all of these lenses, which option best addresses the situation?
8. If I told someone I respect (or a public audience) which option I have chosen, what would they say?
9. How can my decision be implemented with the greatest care and attention to the concerns of all stakeholders?

Implement Your Decision and Reflect on the Outcome

10. How did my decision turn out, and what have I learned from this specific situation? What (if any) follow-up actions should I take?

This framework for thinking ethically is the product of dialogue and debate at the Markkula Center for Applied Ethics at Santa Clara University. Primary contributors include Manuel Velasquez, Dennis Moberg, Michael J. Meyer, Thomas Shanks, Margaret R. McLean, David DeCosse, Claire André, Kirk O. Hanson, Irina Raicu, and Jonathan Kwan. It was last revised on November 5, 2021.

APPENDIX B

CODES OF CAMPAIGN CONDUCT

Campaign codes of conduct are increasingly being recommended or adopted by professional organizations and governments. Here are a few examples.

AAPC Code of Professional Ethics

As a member of the American Association of Political Consultants, I believe there are certain standards of practice which I must maintain. I, therefore, pledge to adhere to the following Code of Professional Ethics:

1. I will not indulge in any activity which would corrupt or degrade the practice of political consulting.
2. I will treat my colleagues and clients with respect and never intentionally injure their professional or personal reputations.
3. I will respect the confidence of my clients and not reveal confidential or privileged information obtained during our professional relationship.
4. I will use no appeal to voters which is based on racism, sexism, religious intolerance or any form of unlawful discrimination and will condemn those who use such practices. In turn, I will work for equal voting rights and privileges for all citizens.
5. I will refrain from false or misleading attacks on an opponent or member of his or her family and will do everything in my power to prevent others from using such tactics.

6. I will document accurately and fully any criticism of an opponent or his or her record.
7. I will be honest in my relationship with the news media and candidly answer questions when I have the authority to do so.
8. I will use any funds I receive from my clients, or on behalf of my clients, only for those purposes invoiced in writing.
9. I will not support any individual or organization which resorts to practices forbidden by this code.
10. I will be committed to a vibrant democracy including ensuring free and fair elections that obey all laws and I will not degrade American Democracy. The continual and peaceful democratic process is central to our profession and a necessary part of our nation.

Source: https://theaapc.org/code-of-ethics/ as of 2/9/24

Institute for Local Government

Pledge of Fair Campaign Practices
There are basic principles of honesty, fairness, responsibility and respect to which every candidate for public office should adhere in order to be worthy of the public office that that candidate seeks. Candidates who fall short of adhering to such principles alienate the public from the electoral process and erode the public's trust and confidence in the offices that those candidates seek.
THEREFORE, as a candidate for public office, I pledge to conform my campaign to the following principles:

1. General

- ☐ My campaign for public office will adhere to principles of honesty, fairness, responsibility and respect.
- ☐ My campaign communications will present only fair, relevant and truthful information to the voters for their consideration of my candidacy and those of my opponents.

2. Fairness.

- ☐ The timing of my communications will be such that my opponents will have a meaningful opportunity to respond to any claims I make concerning their positions or qualifications to hold office.
- ☐ I will not take advantage of any position I hold in the public, private or nonprofit sectors to pressure people to support my candidacy with either campaign contributions or other election help.

3. Relevance.

- ☐ Irrelevant information includes appeals to prejudices based on race, sex, sexual preferences, religion, national origin, physical health status, or age, as well as information concerning the candidate's family.

4. Truthfulness.

- ☐ I will present my positions and record candidly and forthrightly, so that the voters can judge my candidacy for office.
- ☐ I will document all assertions my campaign makes in campaign communications.

5. Responsibility.

- ☐ I support full participation in the electoral process and will take no action to discourage such participation.
- ☐ I will immediately and publicly repudiate those who take actions that either help my candidacy or hurt my opponents' candidacy which are inconsistent with this pledge of campaign conduct.

6. Respect.

- ☐ I will treat my opponents with courtesy and civility, even when we disagree about what is best for voters served by the office I seek.

Source: available as of 2/9/24 at:
https://www.ca-ilg.org/sites/main/files/file-attachments/resources__Pledge_of_Fair_Campaign_Practices.pdf?1436996318

APPENDIX C

A NON-EXHAUSTIVE LIST OF ETHICAL QUESTIONS CANDIDATES MIGHT FACE ON THE CAMPAIGN TRAIL

Ethical Dilemmas Involving Honesty

- ☐ Are you truthful about your record, background, and accomplishments?
- ☐ Are you truthful about your opponent's record, background, accomplishments, or malfeasance?
- ☐ Do you ensure that campaign staff, consultants, surrogates, or others speaking on your behalf are always truthful?
- ☐ Do you imply endorsements where none have been given?
- ☐ Do you Photoshop images or use "deepfakes" to enhance messages that are not entirely truthful?
- ☐ Are you honest about what you can and will do once in office?
- ☐ Do you deceive the public by using push polling to deliver campaign messages under the guise of legitimate research?
- ☐ Are you honest about the signatures you have gathered?
- ☐ Do you report truthfully on all campaign reports?
- ☐ Are you honest about your relationships with Independent Expenditure Groups?
- ☐ Are your answers on political questionnaires consistent?

Ethical Dilemmas Involving Fairness

- ☐ Even if an allegation against an opponent is true, is it fair under the circumstances? For example, did the alleged event occur in the distant past?
- ☐ Are you distorting your opponent's voting record by taking a vote out of context? For example, does your opponent have a favorable record on an issue, but voted for a necessary appropriation bill that included a section not favorable on that issue?
- ☐ Are negative allegations against your opponent relevant to the office being sought? For example, do allegations against the opponent's family further the political debate or only serve to demean the opponent in the public's view?
- ☐ Do you buy up the majority of available airtime, thus drowning out the voices of your opponents?
- ☐ Do you hire more political consultants than necessary, thus ensuring that they cannot work for your opponent?
- ☐ When making a negative comment about your opponent, do you give your opponent reasonable time to respond, or do you hold information back, planning for an "October surprise"?
- ☐ If you are already an officeholder, do you use public resources not available to your opponent? For example, do you use government staff, offices, supplies and/or equipment for political purposes?
- ☐ As an officeholder, do you use governmental meetings as an opportunity to campaign?
- ☐ Do you encourage or condone the destruction of your opponent's campaign materials by staff and/or volunteers?
- ☐ Do you interfere with the voting process by discouraging voter turnout?

Ethical Dilemmas Involving Transparency

- ☐ Do you make all your responses to special interest questionnaires publicly available?
- ☐ Do you disclose all your donors in compliance with campaign finance regulations?
- ☐ Do you disclose financial interests?
- ☐ Do you provide your tax returns when asked?
- ☐ Do you disclose promises made to donors and supporters?
- ☐ Do you disclose when you or your campaign are using artificial intelligence in advertising, outreach, or fundraising?

Ethical Dilemmas Involving Substance

- ☐ Have you developed policy positions on the issues facing the electorate?
- ☐ Do you provide the public with access to all your policy positions?
- ☐ Do you honor requests to debate?
- ☐ Do your allegations about your opponent(s) serve to educate the public about your differences or do they merely serve to attack your opponent?
- ☐ Are your political advertisements mere fluff pieces or do they actually inform the voters about your stance on the issues?
- ☐ Do you conduct political town hall meetings so your views can be made known?
- ☐ Do you stand open to questions from your future constituents?
- ☐ Do you respond to emails and other correspondence from voters?
- ☐ Do you answer questions from the press and participate in editorial board meetings?

Ethical Dilemmas Involving Independence

- ☐ Do you pre-commit yourself by promising that you will take positions on legislation prior to having the benefit of public hearings and proper governmental deliberation? For example, do you make promises in your responses to campaign questionnaires that bind you to a certain course of action once elected? Do you sign pledges?
- ☐ Do you make promises to donors in exchange for contributions?
- ☐ Do you make promises to supporters in exchange for endorsements?
- ☐ Do you exercise your own judgment when devising policy or do you feel you must be in lockstep with your party in order to get party support?
- ☐ Do you take donations from a group that has business before you if you are an incumbent or will likely have business before you, should you get elected? For example, if you are running for a seat on the city council, do you take money from developers?

Ethical Dilemmas Involving Campaign Contributions

- ☐ As campaign finance laws are designed to eliminate corruption and undue influence, do you follow all pertinent campaign finance laws and regulations?
- ☐ If you are given funds in excess of contribution limits, do you return them or do you work with the donor to circumvent the campaign finance rules? For example, do you advise the donor to divide up the funds among family members who then donate to you?

- ☐ Do you directly, or indirectly, coordinate with independent groups campaigning on your behalf?
- ☐ Do you send former political staffers to work on independent expenditure committees?
- ☐ If you are an incumbent, do you seek contributions from government staff?
- ☐ If you are in business, do you seek contributions for your political campaign from your employees?

This appendix was updated from its original source: Hana Callaghan, *Campaign Ethics; A Field Guide,* Markkula Center for Applied Ethics, 2019. https://www.scu.edu/government-ethics/resources/campaign-ethics-a-field-guide/

APPENDIX D

ADDITIONAL RESOURCES

Artificial Intelligence (AI) in Elections and Campaigns, National Conference of State Legislatures
https://www.ncsl.org/elections-and-campaigns/artificial-intelligence-ai-in-elections-and-campaigns

Ballotpedia
https://ballotpedia.org/

Brennan Center for Justice
https://www.brennancenter.org/

Campaign Legal Center
https://www.campaignlegalcenter.org

Center on Civility & Democratic Engagement
https://gspp.berkeley.edu/centers/ccde

Citizens for Responsibility and Ethics in Washington
https://www.citizensforethics.org

Democracy Docket
https://www.democracydocket.com/

Federal Election Commission
https://www.fec.gov/

Fact Check
https://www.factcheck.org/

Maplight
https://www.maplight.org/

Markkula Center for Applied Ethics
https://www.scu.edu/ethics/

Note: All of these web links were available as of February 9, 2024

www.ingramcontent.com/pod-product-compliance
Lightning Source LLC
LaVergne TN
LVHW012023060526
838201LV00061B/4425